Urban Policy and Economic Development
An Agenda for the 1990s

Urban Policy and Economic Development
An Agenda for the 1990s

A
World
Bank
Policy
Paper

The World Bank
Washington, D.C.

Cover design by Beni Chibber-Rao
Desktop publishing by Michelle Lynch Zook
Photos by John M. Courtney

ISBN 0-8213-1816-0
ISSN 1014-8124

Contents

Acknowledgments

The principal author of this paper was Michael A. Cohen, Chief of the Urban Development Division; Kyu Sik Lee, Louis Pouliquen, and James O. Wright, Jr. contributed to the development of the policy and analytical framework and the paper's overall structure and line of argument. Robert Buckley, Per Ljung, and Stephen Mayo contributed to earlier versions of the paper. The paper benefited from contributions from the staff of the Urban Development Division and the Operations Complex. Luisa Victorio and Armi Felix provided secretarial support.

Urban Policy and Economic Development
An Agenda for the 1990s

Executive Summary

Rapid demographic growth will add 600 million people to cities and towns in developing countries during the 1990s, about two-thirds of the expected total population increase. Of the world's 21 megacities, which will expand to have more than 10 million people, 17 will be in developing countries. With urban economic activities making up an increasing share of GDP in all countries, the productivity of the urban economy will heavily influence economic growth.

This paper analyzes the fiscal, financial, and real sector linkages between urban economic activities and macroeconomic performance. It builds on this analysis to propose a policy framework and strategy that will redefine the urban challenge in developing countries:

- First, the developing countries, the international community, and the World Bank should move toward a broader view of urban issues, a view that moves beyond housing and residential infrastructure, and that emphasizes the productivity of the urban economy and the need to alleviate the constraints on productivity.
- Second, with urban poverty increasing, the productivity of the urban poor should be enhanced by increasing the demand for labor and improving access to basic infrastructure and social services.
- Third, more attention should be devoted to reversing the deterioration of the urban environment, an issue receiving short shrift in the face of global environmental problems.
- Fourth, the serious gap in understanding urban issues must be closed. With the decline in urban research during the 1980s, few countries have a sound analytical basis for urban policy.

How are the World Bank and the international community responding to these challenges? Past urban operations focused on neighborhood interventions—such as sites and services and slum upgrading during the 1970s and municipal development and housing finance during the 1980s. Assessments of this assistance conclude that citywide impacts have been rare and that the pace of urban growth far exceeded the scale of the urban program. Today, there is a need to focus urban operations on citywide policy reform, institutional development, and high-priority investments— and to put the development assistance in the urban sector in the context of broader objectives of economic development and macroeconomic performance.

The Challenge of Urban Growth

Since 1950 the world's urban population has grown from under 300 million to 1.3 billion persons, with unrelenting annual growth of 4 percent, adding 45-50 million persons a year. Growth rates of smaller towns have been even higher as non-farm employment has supported agricultural growth. While urban settlement patterns have varied across countries, in no country have efforts to restrain migration or urban growth been successful. Secondary cities such as Kano, Surabaya, or Guadalajara have become metropolitan areas. Today, natural increase has replaced migration as the major source of urban growth in most continents except Africa.

The forces contributing to urban growth are strong. Higher urban wages reflect the higher productivity of labor in cities where economies of scale and agglomeration have made households and enterprises more productive. This productivity growth, although beneficial, has not solved the massive urban problems of the developing world, and serious issues of urban poverty and a deteriorating urban environment remain. Many households have not found employment and income-generating activities, and many live in squatter areas unserved by essential infra-structure. In 1988 some 330 million urban residents—about a quarter of the total urban population—lived in poverty. Even if poverty is still largely rural in many countries, as the 1990 *World Development Report* concludes, urban poverty will become the most significant and politi-cally explosive problem in the next century.

Past Government Efforts and Donor Assistance

Since 1972 government efforts, particularly those supported by donors, have addressed urban growth and urban poverty through low-cost investment projects in shelter, water supply, sanitation, and urban transport. Sites-and-services and slum-upgrading projects were in-tended to demonstrate replicable approaches that could provide benefits to the poor while recovering costs and reducing the financial burden on the public sector. Many of these projects were reasonably successful in meeting their physical project objectives; this required devoting attention to physical implementation rather than sustaining policy change and strengthening institutions. As a result, they have not had major impact on the policies of national and local governments and the broader issues of managing the urban economy. In only a few cases, such as the Kampung Improvement Program in Jakarta, have citywide impacts been achieved. Most important, because many urban programs did not achieve sustainable policy reform and institutional development, they were not replicable. Government and donor programs tended to divide a city into projects, improving specific neighborhoods without improving the urban policy and institutional framework such as the functioning of citywide markets for land and housing. Government efforts have not mobilized the private sector and community initiative, but in many cases have increased the cost of private solutions through overregulation and the rationing of scarce capital for investment.

From a broader perspective, several additional conclusions come from assessing past efforts. First, it is apparent that neither governments nor donors have sought to understand the impacts of macroeconomic policy on urban economic activities. Second, those institutions and experts working within the urban sector have not appreciated the impact of their activities on macroeconomic performance. A third dimension of this narrow perspective on the relationships between the macroeconomic and urban levels is the absence of discussion of short- versus long-term impacts of policies at one level on the other. Finally, one of the most glaring deficiencies of previous efforts has been the insufficient attention given to the issue of productivity within the urban economy. The policy framework presented in this paper seeks to address these weaknesses of previous urban policy. It also seeks to incorporate the issues of increasing urban poverty and a growing urban environmental crisis within this broader perspective.

A New Policy Framework: The Urban Economy and Macroeconomic Performance

The policy framework developed in this paper distinguishes between macroeconomic policies that are managed at the national level and urban policies that are largely, though not exclusively, managed at the city level. Macroeconomic policies establish the broad economic environment for urban economic activities. They affect interest rates, direct and indirect taxes, incentives for manufacturing and trade, and the pricing of key inputs such as energy and water. The financing of national fiscal deficits absorbs credit needed for productive investment, while also increasing interest rates and contributing to inflation. Trade incentives have direct impacts on urban production, concentrating industrial investment and adding to the growth of port cities. Similarly, national strategies for education and health have direct consequences for the quality of the urban labor force. Achieving the long-term objective of improving the productivity of the urban economy thus depends heavily on the successful balancing of the many parts of macroeconomic policy.

The performance of the urban economy also affects macroeconomic performance. Three linkages—financial, fiscal, and real sector—produce significant urban impacts at the macroeconomic level. The weak condition of the financial sector in most developing countries, and particularly its difficulty in mobilizing private savings, has left most of the financing of urban investments to the public sector. Since the spending of local and provincial governments, coupled with residential capital investment by households, accounts for 10-15 percent of GDP and 30-40 percent of fixed capital formation in the urbanized countries of Latin America, the financing of these investments can contribute to the widespread financial distress in these countries. The fiscal linkage between the urban economy and the macroeconomy is equally important: poor local government revenue performance contributes to the consolidated budget deficit at the national level. Similarly, the absence of means to mobilize private savings for housing has resulted in large public subsidies for housing. Local government expenditures can also destabilize fragile fiscal balances. In the real sector, constraints on productivity at the city level such as infrastructure deficiencies reduce the productivity of firms and households and thus reduce the aggregate productivity of the economy.

Within this perspective, better macroeconomic management over the long term is needed to establish the parameters for urban economic growth. At the same time, the short-term disruptions in orderly macroeconomic growth have important consequences for cities. Structural adjustment policies at the macro level are intended over the longer term to create an enabling policy environment for more productive urban economies. Such an environment would increase the efficiency of firms and households and would thus support the economywide adjustment and the resumption of growth. For many countries, however, these policy changes require a corresponding urban adjustment to support national economic adjustment goals. Such a process should result in more flexible institutional and regulatory regimes at the city level to adjust to new macroeconomic realities. It would affect the production of goods and services and the broad context for investment, savings, resource mobilization, and capital formation in urban areas.

Improving Urban Productivity

The increased importance of the urban economic activities in national production requires greater effort to improve their productivity. But improved macroeconomic management is only a necessary but not sufficient condition to improve productivity at the city level. Macroeconomic policy must also take into account the spatial dimensions of the urban economy. Economies of scale and agglomeration economies are the benefits of the concentration of urban population and economic activities; however, these economies also have costs. Key constraints such as infrastructure deficiencies, the regulatory framework governing urban markets for land and housing, weak municipal institutions, and inadequate financial services for urban development all affect these spatial dimensions and limit the productivity of firms and households in producing goods and services. The cumulative effect of these constraints is to reduce the productivity of the urban economy and its contribution to macroeconomic performance.

Infrastructure deficiencies seriously constrain the productivity of private investment in most cities in developing countries. Firms must invest significant shares of their capital in private electric power generation. Traffic congestion impedes the movement of goods and services and thus reduces the economies of agglomeration of urban markets. Some cities have more cars than telephones, while the unreliable water supplies in other urban areas constrain manufacturing. Inadequate public collection and disposal of vast quantities of solid waste add to the deterioration of air, water, and land. These public infrastructure services constitute needed *intermediate* inputs to economic activities. If such services are unavailable, private enterprises are forced to provide them on their own. That increases their total investment requirements and constrains the productivity of that investment—reducing the growth of profits, incomes, and employment, and raising prices.

A second major constraint is the heavy cost of inappropriate urban regulatory policies. Regulations affecting the establishment of productive activities significantly hinder the speed and efficiency of investment. Lengthy procedures to obtain construction permits impose heavy additional costs. Other regulations, such as those governing the markets for land and housing, have less direct, but nevertheless significant impacts on productivity by decreasing the costs of industrial and commerical investment and inputs needed for production

A third constraint on urban productivity is the weakness of municipal institutions, both financial and technical. The dominant role of central government in planning and financing urban infrastructure has starved local governments for financial resources. The recent financial crisis has made this situation worse, especially in Latin America where previously well-established municipal institutions have withered in the absence of central government financial transfers. In a 1984 survey of 86 developing countries, property taxes averaged less than 1 percent of total revenue. And in 19 countries between 1978 and 1986, the deficits of subnational governments (provincial and municipal) accounted on average for half the consolidated government deficit, and thus a significant percentage of GDP.

Financial dependency on central governments also affects the operation of local governments. Central control over the public investment process has undermined local commitment and capacities to operate and maintain public infrastructure and services, directly affecting the efficiency of resource use. The failure to maintain infrastructure has reached crisis proportions, and maintenance has become a developmental priority.

A fourth constraint on urban productivity is the inadequacy of financial services for urban development. Poorly developed financial sectors constrain investment in infrastructure, housing, and other urban economic activities. Weak financial systems are unable to mobilize private savings and lead governments to use public resources to finance housing. The links between the financial sector and the urban economy go in both directions, as pressure for financial subsidies in housing can have macro-financial effects.

These constraints on urban productivity matter more as urban economic activities have made up a growing share of GDP in developing countries. In the short term, the resumption of economic growth will depend in part on alleviating these constraints. In the long term, the economic future of urbanized countries will be closely linked to the level and growth of the productivity of their urban economies. While the stakes are of national significance, reducing these constraints will depend heavily on local policies and institutions, such as those for managing local fiscal deficits.

To increase the productivity of the urban economy and ensure its contribution to macroeconomic performance requires actions at the national and city levels to reduce these constraints on urban productivity. Achieving this objective will require sustained policy reform and increased efforts to strengthen urban institutions. It will involve a shift in the role of central governments from direct providers of urban services and infrastructure to "enablers," creating a regulatory and financial environment in which private enterprises, households, and community groups can play an increasing role in meeting their own needs. It will also require some measure of decentralization of responsibility to municipalities for urban finance and the management of infrastructure, with adequate safeguards to ensure accountability. This will be a complex and politically difficult process, requiring establishing a productive and sustainable balance between local autonomy and central control.

The strategy for loosening the constraints on urban productivity has four elements which apply to regional cities of different sizes as well as the capital city:

- Strengthening the management of urban infrastructure at the city level—by improving the level and composition of investment, reinforcing the institutional capacity for operation and maintenance, and seeking opportunities for greater private sector involvement.
- Improving the citywide regulatory framework to increase market efficiency and to enhance the private sector's provision of shelter and infrastructure.
- Improving the financial and technical capacity of municipal institutions through more effective division of resources and responsibilities between central and local governments.
- Strengthening financial services for urban development.

Alleviating Urban Poverty

Despite the efforts of governments and donors, the numbers of urban poor continue to increase as a result of demographic growth and constraints on productivity, and therefore on the growth of employment and incomes, and constrained access to services. The physical manifestations of urban poverty are evident in all cities in developing countries: vast neighborhoods of squatters—*barriadas, bidonvilles,* and *bustees*—living outside the legal framework of the city, lacking water, sanitation, urban transport, and adequate shelter, and unserved by social services such as health and education. Poor quality of life is worsened further amidst a deteriorating local environment.

Although serious in all countries, urban poverty has become particularly problematic in countries undergoing macroeconomic adjustment. Reduced subsidies to food, water, transport, and energy in urban areas, coupled with the shifting demand for labor and transitional unemployment, have reduced urban real incomes. Lower-middle class groups have been affected most, pushed into the lower-income category until the resumption of growth leads to improved opportunities for employment, higher productivity, and increased wages. These social costs of adjustment have been particularly visible in the political arena.

Three broad channels link adjustment to the incidence of poverty:

- *Wages.* Since the urban poor are especially dependent on their labor, rather than asset ownership, they bear the greatest risk when unemployment rises. Restrictive monetary and fiscal policies affect the urban poor by shrinking labor demand.

- *Prices.* Wages adjust much more slowly than the prices of goods and services as adjustment reduces absorption, and as currency devaluations impose upward pressure on import prices. Whereas the rural poor might derive some benefit from exchange devaluation, the urban poor are net losers. In addition, fiscal reform usually involves real increases in tariffs, which again tend to affect the urban poor disproportionately.
- *Public services.* Cuts in public expenditure are usually a necessary component of adjustment programs, including reductions in public health or education which tend to have disproportionate impacts on the poor.

Managing these links between macroeconomic developments and impacts on the urban poor are important on both equity and efficiency grounds. Supporting the productive contribution of the urban poor to the urban economy will require an appropriate strategy to stimulate the demand for labor while ensuring, through provision of adequate social services and infrastructure, that the poor can take advantage of the opportunities provided. It also requires a safety net for the most vulnerable.

The challenge of urban management in the economic environment of the 1990s is to improve productivity while directly alleviating the growing incidence of urban poverty, and thereby also improving equity. As *World Development Report 1990* spells out, this does not require a trade-off between strategies to promote economic growth and to reduce poverty; poverty reduction is possible in part through improving productivity at the individual, household, firm, and urban levels. This approach involves directly increasing the labor intensity of productive investment and improving the human capital of the poor through better education, health, and nutrition.

To alleviate urban poverty—due to the short-term impacts of macroeconomic adjustment and the longer-term structural problems of demographic growth, low productivity, and constrained access to urban services—requires:

Managing the economic aspects of poverty, through—

- Increasing the demand for the labor of the poor through government policies to encourage labor-intensive productive activities.
- Alleviating the structural constraints inhibiting the productivity and growth of the informal sector by reforming regulations and codes that limit the access of the poor to urban services, infrastructure, credit, and markets.
- Increasing the labor productivity of the poor by reducing constraints preventing labor-force participation, such as constraints

on women's time, including childcare and other family responsibilities.

Managing the social aspects of poverty, through—

- Increasing social-sector expenditure for human-resource development of the urban poor by providing basic services in education, health, nutrition, family planning, and vocational training.
- Increasing the access of the poor to infrastructure and housing to meet their basic needs.
- Recognizing and supporting the efforts of the poor to meet their own needs through community initiatives and local, nongovernmental organizations.

Targeting "safety net" assistance to those most vulnerable to short-term shocks, such as women who head households, through—

- Directing transfers in food assistance, health care, employment, and provision of other basic needs on a short-term basis.
- Introducing measures to moderate the decline in private consumption.

Protecting the Urban Environment

The third area requiring attention is the emerging environmental crisis in towns and cities, a problem receiving far less attention than that going to such global environmental issues as global warming or the scarcity of water resources. Urban environmental problems add much to these global problems because of the intensity of energy and resource use and the concentration of wastes and emissions. However, while the impacts of global problems are long-term, the impacts of urban environmental problems are also short-term. These impacts on the health and productivity of individuals, households, and communities are immediate—from congestion, air and water pollution, inadequate sanitation, erratic waste collection and disposal, and the destruction of marginal lands. In 1987, less than 60 percent of the urban population had access to adequate sanitation, and only one-third was connected to sewer systems. The impacts on local environments are visible and dangerous.

The main health risks from environmental degradation are those from pathogens in the environment, indoor air pollution, substandard housing, and industrialization. Deaths and illnesses from gastroenteric and respiratory diseases are closely linked to substandard housing and infrastructure. Diarrhea and respiratory infections are leading killers of infants in the least developed countries. Acute respiratory infections in children and chronic bronchitis in women are closely linked to inadequate housing and especially smoke exposure. Air pollution and exposure to toxic chemicals also exact a heavy health toll.

Environmental degradation also has long-term effects on resources, threatening not only human health and ecosystems but also the sustainability of development. Groundwater depletion or contamination can be serious, as can the loss of land resources when the development of wetlands, coastal zones, or erosion prone areas is not controlled. Hazardous industrial wastes are another major concern, since it is difficult to monitor discharges and ensure that they are not put into sewers or landfills—and since few developing countries have the facilities needed to treat and dispose of hazardous wastes. And many environmental problems with national and international implications— such as emissions of carbon dioxide, sulphur dioxide, and nitrous oxide—have their origin in urban industry and transport.

Despite these local problems, they are poorly understood in developing countries and require a major research and development effort to identify effective approaches to their solution. To develop sustainable approaches to the management of the urban environment requires:

- Raising global awareness of the urban environmental crisis, in order to develop the political support for action.
- Improving the information base and understanding of the dynamics of environmental deterioration in urban areas.
- Developing city-specific urban environmental strategies that respond to the circumstances of individual cities.
- Identifying programs of curative action for cities to redress the most serious environmental consequences of past public policies and private behavior.
- Formulating effective national and urban policies and incentives to prevent further environmental deterioration.

Increasing Understanding of Urban Issues

After extensive investments in urban research during the 1970s, the quantity of urban research fell sharply in developed and developing countries in the 1980s. The scarcity of public resources for universities and independent research institutes, coupled with increasing interest in such other subjects as debt and adjustment, has led to a decline in urban research capacity just when many urban policy questions are becoming increasingly important. The need is thus great for increasing research on urban issues. The priority areas for research include the linkages between the urban economy and macroeconomic aggregates, the internal efficiencies of cities and urban productivity, the urban poor and the informal sector, the financing of urban investments, the role of government in the urban development process, and the urban environment. In response to this situation, the Ford Foundation is undertaking an assessment of urban research in the developed and developing countries during 1991–92. This assessment will be the basis for discussion in 1992 of international support for urban research.

Implementing the New Agenda

While the World Bank and the international community cannot be expected to fully satisfy the enormous demands from developing countries for assistance in the urban sector, a major external effort should be made to increase local capacity in the 1990s to address these needs. The proposed agenda, with much greater emphasis on national and city-wide policies and institutional development is going to be much more costly, especially in terms of up-front policy analysis and institutional development. These types of activities have been funded increasingly by bilateral agencies and UNDP-financed, Bank-executed programs such as the Urban Management Program. This program and other bilateral and multilateral initiatives should help meet technical assistance needs.

In response to the requests of member countries and heightened appreciation of urban problems in the regions, the World Bank's urban activities are expected to grow. Increased assistance will be accompanied by an intensified effort to improve the impact of lending by explicitly reorienting its emphasis through policy and institutional development in most countries. Bank urban lending will shift from provision of neighborhood investments in shelter infrastructure to national and city level policy reform, institutional development, and infrastructure investments to support a country's overall development. These operations will focus on improving the national and city level policy and institutional frameworks and will involve increased policy content; for example, reform of central-local financial relations as part of strengthening municipal institutions or regulatory reform as an integral part of lending for housing finance. Public sector investments in infrastructure will continue but include support for operations and maintenance at the city level, as well as rehabilitation where needed to maintain the reliability of services. The analytical foundations of urban assistance will also be strengthened, including assessments of land and housing markets, regulatory audits, and analysis of central-local financial relations.

An appreciation of the economic and political significance of urbanization in the developing countries is emerging slowly in the private sector, the official donor community, and the Bank itself. This appreciation is reflected in growing lending programs, increasing requests for urban assistance to bilateral agencies, and the proliferation of discussions in many fora of urban infrastructure, environmental issues, and growing movements of citizen involvement in the solution of local problems.

Introduction

As urban assistance by the World Bank and the international community grows in response to the growing demand of developing countries, the need arises to assess the impact of past and ongoing operations in light of the broader challenges facing developing countries in the 1990s. Growing concern about urban poverty and environmental degradation heightens the need for a strategy that will integrate these issues within the framework of development policy.

Economic crises of the past decade have brought on an increasing urgency to correct past economic distortions and thus improve longer term prospects for growth. The World Bank *Report on Structural Adjustment Lending II* has identified the short-term need for policy reform and public investment to stimulate private investment and improve productivity. This paper looks at ways to alleviate the constraints on the productivity of the urban economy—productivity that accounts for a large share of gross domestic product (GDP) in most countries. It examines the effect of those constraints on urban productivity and thus on macroeconomic performance.

The demographic and environmental pressures of urbanization in developing countries intensified during the past decade giving new significance to the effects of urban growth in the 1990s. As cities and towns continue to grow rapidly, urban populations are reaching unprecedented sizes. The growth increases pressures on environmental resources; this in turn affects the access of the poor to water supply, clean air, habitable land, and sanitation. Cities are the locus of productive economic activities and hope for the future, yet they face growing environmental problems and increasing poverty. In 1988, fully 25 percent of the urban population—some 330 million people—lived in poverty.

The stakes for effective policy at the city level have increased—and requests for external assistance have grown—but the record of past efforts is not one of success. Government responses to urban growth have followed the central planning models of the postwar period, with the public sector seeking to control urban investment rather than mobilizing private resources. Inappropriate policies and weak urban institutions have in many cases constrained rather than improved the productivity of cities. Inefficient regulation, inadequate financial services, and serious deficiencies in infrastructure have limited the productivity of firms and households.

Donor assistance to the urban sector has similarly had only a small impact. Urban assistance since the early 1970s has concentrated on the public provision of shelter and residential infrastructure and only more recently on municipal development and housing finance. While these efforts have succeeded in physical terms, they have not achieved citywide or sectorwide policy or institutional impacts. Rather, they have tended to "projectize" the city at the neighborhood level. External assistance has not addressed the major constraints on the urban economy and the need for policy reform suggested above. What is needed then is a change in the objectives of external assistance in the urban sector. Such assistance should focus on the policy and institutional requirements for improving the productivity of the urban economy.

This paper proposes a policy framework and strategy for the improvement of urban productivity, the alleviation of urban poverty, and improved management of the urban environment. Chapter I sets the context by identifying the economic basis for continuing urban growth and by assessing the legacy of government and donor efforts. Chapter II introduces a framework for analysis and policy that focuses on the key constraints to urban productivity, the persistence and increase of urban poverty, and the growing crisis of the urban environment. Chapter III proposes an agenda of policy reform and action for the developing countries, and Chapter IV presents a broadened strategy for the World Bank.

1

The Challenge of Urban Growth

The Economic Basis of Urban Growth

Over the past thirty years, the developing countries have been transformed from a world of villages to a world of cities and towns. Since 1950 the urban population of the developing world has grown from under 300 million to 1.3 billion persons. Annual growth rates of four percent have added 45 to 50 million new urban residents, as all countries in all regions have experienced sustained urbanization.

Projected demographic trends indicate continuing urban growth, with an additional 600 million people living in urban areas by the year 2000. In 1960 Shanghai was the only city in the developing world with more than 10 million persons; by the end of the century, 17 megacities will have reached that size. Mexico City and Sao Paulo are projected to grow to 25 million people—a number equal to the entire world's urban population at the dawn of the industrial revolution in 1750. While most attention has focused on the high growth rates of megacities, the process has affected cities and towns of all sizes. Cities such as Kano, Surabaya, and Guadalajara have become major metropolises over the past decade, reaching the 2 to 3 million level and continuing to grow explosively.

The concentration of people in urban locations has important social and political consequences, but it is above all an economic phenomenon. Rural-urban migration during the 20th century, starting in Latin America well before World War II and accelerating in Asia and Africa in the 1960s, has resulted from both push and pull factors. Increasing agricultural productivity has reduced the growth in demand for rural labor, while urban areas offer better prospects for jobs and higher incomes. Migrants have tended to come from the bottom and the top of the rural income distribution: the landless and rural poor often have no choice but to seek their livelihood off the farm, whereas the successful farmers frequently use their surpluses to finance the move to nearby towns and later to large urban centers.

Figure 1. Population in Developing Countries

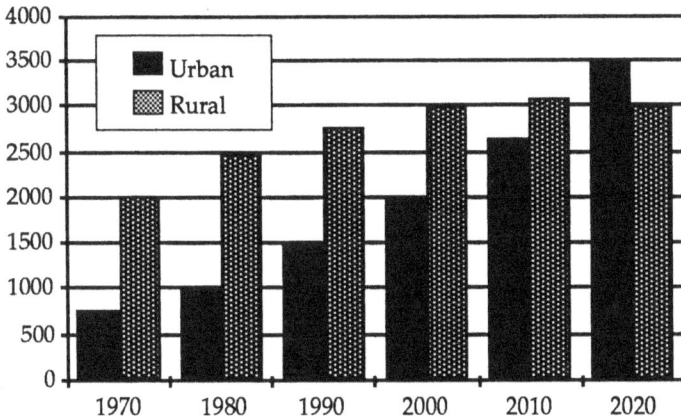

Source: UN: *The Prospects of World Urbanization, 1987.*

The hopes of migrants have largely been met in urban areas. Higher wages and incomes reflect the greater productivity of labor supported by economies of scale and agglomeration. Markets for labor, capital, and technology are able to exploit locational economies (sometimes referred to as agglomeration economies or externalities; see box 1), translating them into higher incomes and employment opportunities. Indeed, higher levels of productivity are found in larger cities, although some of this productivity reflects the earlier "urban bias" of the 1960s and 1970s when many governments concentrated public investments in large cities. These investments were also complemented by public policies that supported subsidies for urban consumption of food, energy, water, and housing and resulted in significant policy-induced distortions in urban markets. This bias was redressed in some countries during the 1980s through adjustment policies that corrected relative prices and shifted the terms of trade toward the rural sector. As is noted in Chapter II, this shift, though necessary, has also had some negative short-term consequences for the urban population.

The location of cities and towns—usually near adequate supplies of water and frequently at strategic locations for transportation, communications, and trade—further supports the growth and productivity of these markets. The performance of macroeconomies, therefore, is closely linked to the productivity of economic activities in cities. At the same time, negative externalities such as traffic congestion and pollution are often the consequences of the population densities found in cities. Both the size and densities of large cities have begun to result in negative externalities so severe that it is reasonable to question whether there are limits to the benefits of agglomeration.

The economic foundations of urbanization have proven to be power-ful in two respects. First, cities work. Despite the many difficulties that may result from population concentration, there is no denying that higher aggregate and per capita incomes occur in more urbanized countries. Indeed, as figure 2 shows, a close correlation exists between national income and degree of urbanization. By 1989 more than half of GDP in most developing countries was generated in cities and towns. About 80 percent of future growth will come from urban economies in highly urbanized countries in Latin America and Asia. The performance of macroeconomies in the 1990s is thus closely linked to the productivity of economic activities in cities.

Second, no country has been effective in restraining rural-urban migration. Even in China, where postrevolutionary policies strove to restrain the growth of cities, such growth has proceeded at a rapid pace. Efforts to improve productivity in the rural areas should of course continue; in some cases such efforts may reduce the incentives for migration. But prospects of higher incomes in urban areas will continue to be greater incentives than the assurance of food and jobs in rural areas. The city has become the locus of economic and social innovation, culture, and political power in most countries. Prospects of further urban growth underline the need for improved urban productivity and management.

Figure 2. Urbanization and Development

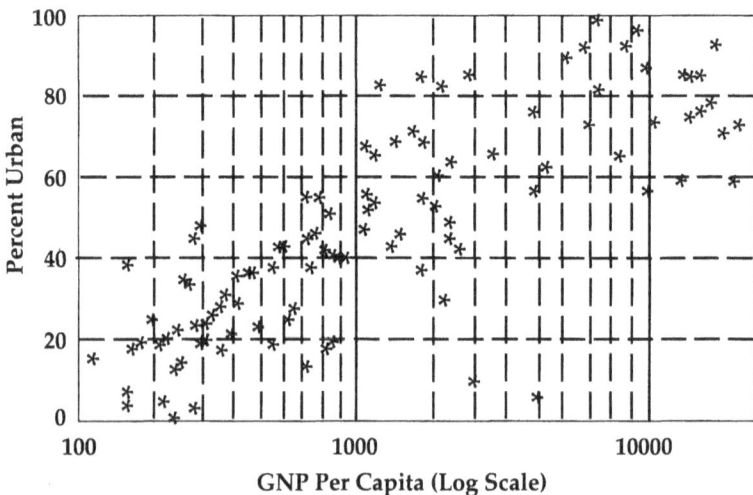

GNP Per Capita (Log Scale)

Source: World Development Report 1988.

Although the growth of urban markets has led to higher aggregate levels of productivity, income, and welfare, it has not been uniformly beneficial for growing urban populations. Many households have prospered in relative terms, but others have been unable to find jobs or to generate incomes sufficient to purchase needed shelter or gain access to urban infrastructure and social services. In most cities, demographic pressures have generated a demand for housing and infrastructure that has increased at a rate far greater than the public sector has been able to satisfy. Public policies have exacerbated this situation by channeling government investment toward the few rather encouraging mobilization of private savings for housing and services for the majority of the population.

By the early 1960s in Latin America and the 1970s in Africa and Asia, modern cities were surrounded by unserviced squatter areas known as favelas, barriadas, or bidonvilles. These settlements housed growing numbers of poor families. Shelter was built by squatters. Water supply was bought from private vendors or collected from wells. Sanitation consisted of on-site latrines. Transportation was provided by informal operators. Social services were minimal. These patterns of settlement were frequently inefficient. They contributed to the degradation of the urban environment through the occupation of marginal land and pollution of water resources. Informal waste disposal contributed to deteriorating health conditions. Thus the effects of rapid demographic growth were often worsened by public policy.

Demographic growth, ineffective policies, and imperfect labor markets have led to growing numbers of poor urban households throughout the developing world. Bank estimates suggest that in 1988 some 330 million urban residents—about 25 percent of the total urban population—lived in poverty. The poorest households most frequently were headed by women. These numbers, coupled with country projections for the future, indicate that even if the global poverty problem is still largely rural in most countries, as the 1990 *World Development Report* concluded, urban poverty will become increasingly serious and politically explosive in the future.

Given the importance of the productivity of urban markets for national economic growth, while directly alleviating the growing incidence of urban poverty, it is important to find specific ways to enhance productivity. However, the policies, investments, and institutions needed to engender higher productivity must be addressed at both the national and local levels. These relationships are presented in Chapter II.

The Pressures of Urban Population Growth

The accelerating demographic pressures of the past thirty years have

Table 1. Urban Growth Patterns

	Country	Per capital GNP level 1988 (US$)	Size of population (in 000's) 1985 Urban	1985 Rural	2000 Urban	2000 Rural	Percentage of urban population 1985	2000	Average rate of growth of — Urban pop. (%) 1980-1985	1995-2000	Rural pop. (%) 1980-1985	1995-2000
Group I	Argentina	2,520	25,648	4,683	32,163	4,075	84.6	88.8	1.88	1.39	-0.87	-0.88
	Mexico	1,760	55,276	24,099	82,985	24,248	69.6	77.4	3.36	2.39	0.34	-0.07
	Colombia	1,180	19,357	9,357	28,557	9,441	67.4	75.2	3.11	2.29	0.28	-0.07
	Brazil	2,160	98,599	36,966	148,397	31,090	72.7	82.7	3.71	2.28	-1.27	-1.00
Group II	Algeria	2,360	9,251	12,448	16,845	16,403	42.6	50.7	3.71	3.85	2.51	1.25
	Morocco	830	9,910	12,210	17,488	13,878	44.8	55.8	4.28	3.42	1.40	0.50
	Malaysia	1,940	5,905	9,543	10,509	10,361	38.2	50.4	4.51	3.32	1.06	0.15
Group III	Senegal	650	2,343	4,101	4,301	5,366	36.4	44.5	3.34	4.26	2.11	1.52
	Ivory Coast	770	4,302	5,950	10,118	8,429	42.0	54.6	6.63	5.24	2.54	2.26
	Nigeria	290	29,556	65,643	68,893	90,256	31.0	43.3	6.07	5.33	2.22	2.02
	Sudan	480	4,502	17,316	8,902	24,708	20.6	26.5	3.99	4.88	2.88	2.19
	Kenya	370	4,002	16,351	11,937	25,645	19.7	31.8	8.06	6.72	3.17	2.78
	Zaire	170	11,248	19,464	22,875	26,474	36.6	46.4	4.41	4.73	2.29	1.80
Group IV	India	340	196,228	572,955	356,875	685,654	25.5	34.2	3.91	3.96	1.65	0.93
	Indonesia	440	42,170	124,294	75,960	132,369	25.3	36.5	4.60	3.62	1.13	0.14
	China	330	218,576	840,946	322,125	963,769	20.6	25.1	1.44	2.95	1.18	0.58

/a/ The World Bank, World Development Indicators, 1990.
/b/ United Nations (Department of International Economic and Social Affairs), Prospects of World Urbanization, 1988.

intensified the challenge of urban growth. Although all countries have experienced urbanization, the rate, magnitude, and character of urban concentration have differed significantly across countries. Table 1 presents four categories of countries, grouped according to (i) their period of most rapid urbanization, (ii) the percentage of urban population, and (iii) present rates of urban growth.

This analysis of urban growth reveals some basic differences in urbanization patterns of the developing countries:

- *Group I:* Heavily urbanized countries of more than 75 percent, with high historical population concentrations, usually including megacities, but declining rates of urban growth. Most growth is attributable to natural increase rather than migration. This type of urban growth is typical in large Latin American countries.
- *Group II:* Recently urbanizing countries, with about half of the population living in urban areas. Population pressures in rural areas will continue to push households to urban areas, but growth rates have peaked and are beginning to decline. This pattern is typical in North African and some Asian countries.
- *Group III:* Primarily rural but rapidly urbanizing countries, experiencing very high urban growth, both in capital cities and secondary towns. Migration continues to be a major source of urban demographic growth, although male migration has been replaced by household migration, leading to a shift toward natural increase as the major fuel of growth. This is typical in many African countries.
- *Group IV:* Large, mostly rural, heavily populated countries with severe pressures on the land. Population size and high growth rates have led to major urban concentrations as well as many secondary cities and towns. Urban growth rates have stabilized at high levels and are projected to continue for the next decade. Large Asian countries fall into this category.

Table 1 indicates significant differences in the rates and magnitudes of urban growth between these categories. Countries in the first category have largely passed their peak urban growth pressure, yet the high national population growth will result in continuing growth of already large cities such as Mexico City, Sao Paulo, and Bogota. This pattern will also extend to smaller centers such as Guadalajara, Recife, and Medellin, that have become major centers of more than 2 million people. These countries face enormous demands for urban employment, infrastructure, and services during a period of continuing macroeconomic crisis. In contrast, cities such as Kuala Lumpur and Tunis in the second category have had more recent urban growth. They have not yet reached megacity proportions. Relatively balanced economic growth has also resulted in development of secondary centers linked to agriculture. This pattern of population distribution is even more pronounced in the third category of countries. In this category, secondary towns have been closely linked to agriculture and served both as market towns and loci of nonfarm employment. The level of urbanization in the fourth category is likely to remain low as a percentage of total population. Countries in this category are characterized by many large cities that perform a range of essential economic functions in support of agriculture, industry, extraction of natural resources, and transportation.

While Table 1 shows differences in the patterns of urban growth, it also reveals important common characteristics across the countries. For example, in most of the four categories, large population concentrations—megacities—have developed—with sizes unprecedented in the developing countries. Although there are historical differences between Mexico City, Sao Paulo, Cairo, Manila, Lagos, Kinshasa, Bombay, Calcutta, Beijing, and Shanghai, each megacity performs major economic functions in its respective country. However, the qualitative implications of their quantitative dimensions (such as the policy and institutional needs of these new urban forms) are not yet understood and will require further analysis.

Figure 3. Population of 20 Large Agglomerations

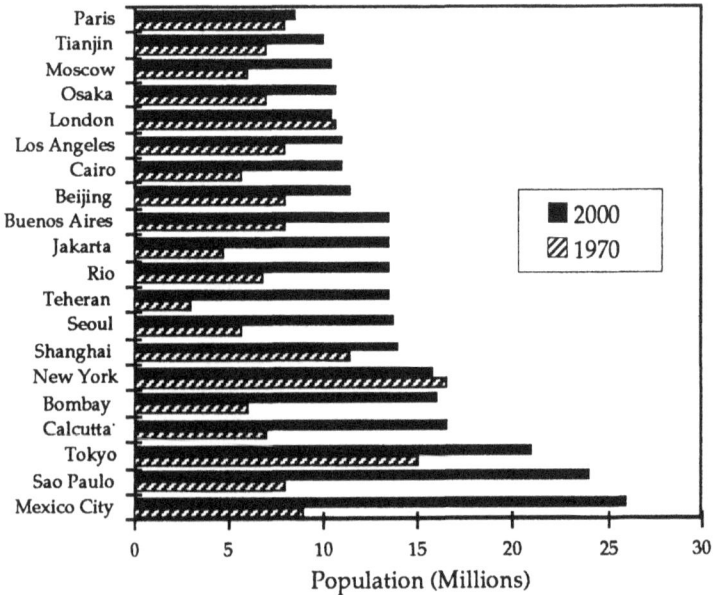

Source: UN: *The Prospects of World Urbanization*, 1987.

Table 2 presents available data on the share of GDP produced by urban areas. A number of inferences can be drawn from the data. First, it is
inconceivable that future economic growth in these countries will not
heavily depend on the productivity of these cities. Second, despite great
differences in levels of GDP and per capita income, each of these
countries has experienced large-scale rural-urban migration, reflecting
better prospects of jobs and of higher incomes in urban areas. Third,
despite the productivity of cities in these countries, there nevertheless
exist serious problems of urban poverty. Finally, few if any of the
countries can claim that their urban environments are not deteriorating
at a rapid rate. All of this suggests that, despite the range of levels of
income, development, or recent economic experience, these countries
share a common set of city-level problems that require policy attention.
These include the need to improve productivity of the urban economy,
to alleviate urban poverty, and to develop sustainable approaches to the
management of the urban environment.

The Need for Management

The major constraints to urban productivity have their origins largely in
the weakness of the public sector. Despite the growing economic and
political importance of cities, the policy and institutional framework for
managing urban growth remains weak. This section assesses both the
efforts of government in this management role and the impact of external
assistance.

Government Efforts

The economic model of the 1960s and 1970s, with a leading role for the
public sector, has also dominated urban policy. The "urban development
model" of the postwar period in most countries has relied on central
government finance and the technical capacity of public agencies. This
has been accentuated by the centralization of political power and a
decline in local government institutions. Control of public investment,
even in large countries such as India and Indonesia, was highly centralized. Urban planning tended to mirror state economic planning, with
public control over most urban activity. Policy focused on public investment. It paid little regard to other critical responsibilities of local institutions, such as operation and maintenance of infrastructure, and establishing incentives required for private economic activities. This public
sector dominance of solutions to the pressures of urban growth has
skewed the range of responses to the provision of shelter and infrastructure. As is noted in Chapter III, the role of government requires redefi-
nition.

Table 2. Some Indicators of the Estimated Economic Importance of Urban Areas

Urban area	Year	Population	Employment	Public revenues	Public expenditures	Output measure
Brazil						36.0 of NDP
Greater Sao Paolo	1970	8.6	"	"	"	48.0 of net industrial product
China						
Shanghai	1980	1.2	"	"	"	12.5 of gross industrial product
Dominican Republic						70.0 of commercial and banking transactions
Santo Domingo	1981	24.0				56.0 of industrial growth
Ecuador						
Guayaquil/a		13.0	"	"	"	30.0 of GDP
Haiti						
All urban	1976	24.2	15.6			57.6 of national income
Port-au-Prince	"	15.0	7.7	47.2	82.7/b	38.7 of national income
Other urban	"	9.2	7.9	"	"	18.9 of national income
India						
All urban	1970/71	19.9	17.7/c	"	"	38.9 of NDP
Kenya						
All urban	1976	11.9	"	"	"	30.3 of income
Nairobi	"	5.2	"	"	"	20.0 of income
Other urban	"	6.7	"	"	"	10.3 of income
Mexico						
All urban	1970	60.0			(29.0)/d	79.7 of personal income
Federal District	"	14.2				33.6 of personal income
Pakistan	1974/75					
Karachi		6.1				16.1 of GDP
Peru						
Lima	1980	28.0				43.0 of GDP
Philippines						
Metro Manilla	1970	12.0	"	45.0		25.0 of GDP
Thailand						
Metro Bangkok	1972	10.9	14.0/e	"	30.5/f	37.4 of GDP
Turkey						
All urban	1981	47.0	42.0			70.0 of GNP
Tunisia						
Tunis	1975	16.0	17.2	"	"	

/a Guayas Province
/b Current expenditures only
/c Workers
/d Federal Public Investment only
/e 1970 data
/f 1969 data

Source: Friedrich Kahnert, "Improving Urban Employment and Labor Productivity."
World Bank Discussion Paper No. 10, May 1987.

Table 3. Sources of Recurrent Municipal Revenue, Selected LCDs
(in percentage)

	Local Taxes/a	Local Fees and Charges	Central Transfers
India	65	10	25
Indonesia	8	9	84
Kenya	39	55	6
Tunisia	32	13	54
Turkey	9	29	62
Brazil	23	9	68
Colombia	44	14	42
Mexico	12	25	64

/a   Includes property taxes collected by central government and returned to municipal governments on the basis of origin.

Note: Excludes receipts from borrowing, and capital grants.

Source: World Bank Sector Studies.

The centralization of the public sector during the 1960s and 1970s is most evident in the changing character of central-local governmental and financial relations. As urban investment needs grew, central governments sought to control the planning and financing of those investments through national building codes and uniform, rather than locally tailored, infrastructure standards as well as through access to investment resources. The philosophy of high standards for urban investment is exemplified by the 1969 statement of an African minister of construction: "Construct big, beautiful, and forever." The task of operation and maintenance was left to local institutions. Central finance and control resulted in a gap between investment and operations. As a consequence, local officials were often not committed to maintaining networks and facilities which they had not designed. Thus maintenance of urban infrastructure has suffered badly, with serious economic consequences that are discussed in Chapter II.

Weak local technical performance has been compounded by limited financial autonomy at the local level. Lacking financial resources under local control, municipalities were unable to attract and retain skilled technical staff. By the late 1970s local governments had become administrative backwaters in most countries, lacking both the financial and technical capacity to fulfill local responsibilities.

The quantitative dimensions of this situation are instructive. The 1988 *World Development Report* concluded that central government transfers constituted about half of local recurrent revenue in most developing countries. In Brazil and Mexico, transfers have represented about two-thirds of local expenditure. Property taxes, the traditional local tax, have generally been less than 25 percent of local revenue and less than 1 percent of total government revenue. In sum, local governments spend, but do not mobilize local resources.

The reluctance of central governments to delegate financial resources and functional responsibilities to municipalities is understandable in political terms. Similarly, political imperatives at the local level militate against municipal taxation. The failure of local institutions to perform is perceived as less damaging in political terms than is an effort to raise local revenues. The overall result is that both central-local relations and strengthening of municipal government are heavily politicized. That makes progress difficult despite the urgent need to respond to the pressures of urban growth. The legacy of government effort, based on assessments in many countries, is unsatisfactory. Institutions are weak, resources are scarce, and technical capacity is inadequate. Those services provided by government— shelter, transport, water supply, and electric power—have tended to benefit a privileged minority rather than serve the majority.

The Impact of External Assistance

As the physical manifestations of urban poverty became increasingly visible by the early 1970s, the international community began to acknowledge urban problems through the launching of various pilot projects. They were intended to demonstrate that the public sector could provide low-cost housing and infrastructure that would be affordable to the urban poor. Public subsidies would be replaced by the mobilization of private savings. Investment costs would be recovered by public agencies. The primary objective was to alleviate urban poverty; a secondary objective was to reduce the financial burden on the public sector for shelter and infrastructure.

These principles were adopted by a number of governments with support from the World Bank and other donors, primarily the United States, the United Kingdom, and France. Sites-and-services projects (the provision of services at affordable standards on sites where households would invest in their own shelter) represented an important break from the conventional subsidized public housing projects. In parallel, the upgrading of squatter areas with infrastructure and other basic needs responded to the poor while also providing environmental improvements. Some 60 sites-and-services and squatter upgrading projects were financed by the Bank during the 1970s. The projects legitimized the rights of the poor to shelter, to infrastructure improvement, and to secure land tenure. Land tenure was viewed as the most critical condition enabling people to invest in their own shelter. The projects also established that the bulldozer should not be used as an instrument of urban policy.

As most of these projects were intended to be pilot in nature, they were supposed to provide replicable models for citywide improvements. They represented an ambitious agenda for policy change and introduction of new approaches for the provision of low-cost services. However, only a few projects were able to reach these proportions. Among them was the Kampung Improvement Project in Jakarta, which reached some 3.6 million people over a 15-year period at a per capita cost of US$37. Similar upgrading schemes were mounted in Calcutta and Madras. However, most efforts, even with second projects, were unable to achieve citywide results. This shortcoming resulted from several factors, including—

- The continuing rapid growth of cities during the project implementation period. The numbers of unserviced settlements in most large cities actually grew during the period. Typically, household formation in the city grew at a faster rate than did shelter construction.
- Insufficient attention to the policy framework for larger-scale and longer-term replicability, including land, housing finance, and municipal finance policies.
- Limited efforts to strengthen the local institutional framework and the local financial base for shelter and infrastructure investment and maintenance.
- Unsustained political commitment to address the problems of the urban poor.

Achievement of physical objectives, including substantial reductions in unit costs of investments in shelter and infrastructure, had absorbed the energy of those involved and had diverted attention from the more difficult areas of sustained policy reform and institutional development.

Despite successful projects in many cities, such as Madras, Mexico City, and Harare, donor assistance has been unable to effectively help governments formulate and implement comprehensive and sustainable urban policies. Instead, cities have become "projectized": rather than develop broader policies for urban land markets, governments of donors have placed emphasis on selection of sites. They have tied infrastructure largely to residential developments, rather than viewing it as an essential input for the productivity of the urban economy.

By the mid-1980s the experiences of donor-assisted projects had led to shifts in external approaches to the urban sector. The central premise of these shifts was the recognition that governments were unable to provide the shelter, infrastructure, and services needed by rapidly growing urban populations. Instead, a more realistic assessment of the capacities of the public sector had led to the conclusion that greater efforts had to be devoted to (i) improving the management of urban institutions, intergovernmental fiscal relations, and a reduced public role in urban service delivery; (ii) improving local resource mobilization; (iii) strengthening the management of urban infrastructure, particularly with regard to maintenance; (iv) establishing regulatory frameworks that were enabling, rather than constraining; and (v) strengthening financial services for urban development.

These shifts in donor approaches to managing urban growth offer the possibility of some notable achievements. These shifts include—

- Greater emphasis on local financial reform, including Bank financing of some 39 projects aimed at improving local tax administration.
- Experiments to establish financing mechanisms for municipal capital expenditures, such as the Third Calcutta Urban Development Project, the Paraná State Market Towns Project, and the Jordan Cities and Villages Development Bank.
- Extensive efforts at strengthening technical capacity for infrastructure maintenance and solid waste collection and disposal.
- Numerous project components to improve land information and registration systems and to introduce regulatory reforms as necessary conditions to improve the functioning of urban land markets.
- Numerous efforts at housing finance reform, including both policies and institutions, in countries such as Mexico, Indonesia, Korea, and Colombia.
- Application of corporate management concepts to city management, such as the Pusan Management Project in Korea.

In most cases it is too early to assess the effects of these recent efforts; in any case, they remain limited in relation to the rate and scale of urban growth. While increasing emphasis on policy and institutional development is urgently needed, it is noteworthy that these efforts have remained within a narrow sectoral view. They have not in most cases been designed with an appreciation of the macroeconomic significance of the management of the urban economy.

In summary, the more recent initiatives of governments and donors reflect a growing appreciation of the importance of policies, institutions, and regulations in formulating effective strategies to manage urban growth. These initiatives reflect an evolution in objectives and have mirrored the shortcomings of government experience. By assuming that government—first central and now local—could provide the investment needed to serve the majority of the urban population, both governments and donors have given little attention to the important role of private households, communities, and firms in providing for their own needs. A need thus exists for a new urban policy framework that is truly enabling for nonpublic actors and realistic in appreciating the relative roles and importance of the public and private sectors. This policy framework must also link the management and productivity of the urban economy to the broader objectives of economic growth and development policy.

2

The Urban Economy and Macroeconomic Performance: A Policy Framework

This chapter presents a policy framework for improving the contribution of cities to economic growth. The productivity of the urban economy is affected by factors that emanate from both national policies and the city level itself. The framework therefore begins by distinguishing between macroeconomic policies, managed at the national level, and urban policies, managed largely, although not exclusively, at the city level. Both levels of policy are embodied in institutional and regulatory frameworks that affect the urban economy. The linkages between the two levels go in both directions: macroeconomic policies affect the city, while urban economic activities have macroeconomic consequences. The chapter then focuses on the specifically "urban" determinants of economic productivity and macroeconomic performance. Among these are the spatial dimensions of the urban economy, including economies of scale and of agglomeration and the positive and negative externalities associated with the location and density of economic activity. These dimensions define and reflect the long-term structure and productivity of urban markets as well as the welfare of the urban population. Application of this policy framework to urban conditions in developing countries leads to the identification of three priority problems facing cities and towns:

- The need to improve the productivity of the urban economy.
- The need to alleviate increasing urban poverty.
- The need to address the growing urban environmental crisis.

The Macroeconomic Context of Urban Growth

Macroeconomic management establishes the economic environment within which urban economic activities occur. Macroeconomic policies affecting interest rates, incentives for manufacturing and trade, pricing of key inputs such as energy and water, and direct and indirect taxation, all directly influence the composition and productivity of urban investment. Financial sector performance and the health of banking systems are critical to industrial expansion and the development of commercial and tertiary services. The financing of national fiscal deficits absorbs credit needed for productive investment, while also increasing interest rates and contributing to inflation. Trade incentives have direct impacts on urban production, as the earlier policies of import substitution demonstrated, by concentrating industrial investment and thus adding to the growth of port cities. Similarly, national strategies for human capital investment through education and health have direct consequences for the quality of the urban labor force. Achieving the long-term objective of improving the productivity of the urban economy thus depends heavily on the successful balancing of the many parts of macroeconomic policy.

One central obstacle to improving aggregate productivity is the pattern of distortions facing different factors of production. One arena that has both benefited and suffered from these distortions are urban markets. The prices of many of the inputs for urban production—labor, capital, infrastructure, energy, and technology—have been affected by economywide distortions. An example is energy pricing that subsidizes imported fuel. Such subvention has resulted in the proliferation of cars and of subsidized private transport in urban areas, thereby creating congestion and air pollution. It also consumes unnecessarily large amounts of foreign exchange. Reducing such distortions is a major task of macroeconomic management. Correcting the distortions can also, in turn, reduce distortions at the urban levels.

The performance of the urban economy also affects macroeconomic performance. Three types of linkages—financial, fiscal, and real sector—can produce significant impacts from the urban to the macroeconomic level. The weak condition of the financial sector in most developing countries, and particularly its difficulty in mobilizing private savings, has meant that the financing of urban investment has weighed heavily on the public sector. In the urbanized countries of Latin America, for example, the expenditures of local and provincial governments, coupled with residential capital investment by households, account for 10 to 15 percent of GDP and 30 to 40 percent of fixed capital formation. The mode of financing of these investments can contribute to the widespread financial distress experienced in these countries. The fiscal linkage between the urban economy and the macroeconomy is equally important: poor local government revenue performance contributes to the consolidated national budget deficit. Similarly, the absence of means to mobilize private savings for housing has resulted in large public subsidies for housing. In Poland, to give one example, the subsidies amount to 5 percent of GDP. Local government expenditures can also destabilize fragile fiscal balances, as the recent decentralization of fiscal control case of Turkey demonstrates. Finally, constraints to productivity at the city

Kano, Nigeria. Government subsidies for basic urban infrastructure, such as water supplies and transport, were cut drastically during the 1980s.

level, such as infrastructure deficiencies presented below, reduce the productivity of firms and households and thus affect the aggregate productivity of the economy.

Short-term disruptions in macroeconomic growth have important consequences for cities. During the 1980s the crises induced by unsustainable domestic fiscal deficits, heavy external debt obligations, and the weight of cumulative economic distortions resulted in the adoption of economic stabilization and adjustment programs in order to restore sustainable macroeconomic balances. These adjustment policies sought to create an enabling policy environment that would increase the efficiency of firms and households and support the economywide adjustment process and the resumption of growth in the long run. A major thrust to these programs has been to encourage a shift toward production of tradables to meet external obligations. At the same time, the programs have had many short run effects on urban economies, firms, and households. At the city level, the following adjustments have occurred:

- To correct relative prices, reduce distortions, and encourage agricultural production, rural-urban terms of trade have shifted in favor of the rural sector.
- To reduce the cost to the government budget, subsidies for urban consumption have been reduced, particularly for food, water, shelter, transport, and energy.
- The relative prices of urban tradable goods (e.g., manufacturing exports) and nontradables (e.g., housing and infrastructure) have changed to the detriment of the latter, making these crucial requirements more costly and more difficult to finance.

- With the shift of urban investment toward tradable goods, the demand for labor has shifted within the urban labor market.
- To mobilize additional resources for investment, urban taxation has been increased.

As has been noted, these adjustments have also involved correcting some of the urban biases inherent in previous government investment programs and pricing policies. Though desirable from a macroeconomic perspective and, indeed, in terms of improving urban productivity, the adjustment process involves costs at the urban level as well as significant risks, which need to be guarded against. Delayed private investment can extend transitional unemployment and postpone the adjustment of labor markets to new industrial incentives. These delays can extend the period of reduced household incomes. If the adjustment process proceeds well, these risks can be minimized. Nonetheless, programs should be considered to cushion the most vulnerable groups from the shocks of adjustment. The consequences on daily urban life have been increasing prices, declining urban real per capita incomes, shifting demand for labor (thus generating unemployment), reduced public expenditure, higher interest rates, and declining public investment—particularly in construction. While these adjustments of structural distortions are needed for longer term productivity and growth, their short term effects have serious political consequences. For example, the outbreaks in Caracas in March 1989 took place in reaction to increases in bus fares, water tariffs, and food prices. Similar recent examples can be found in Cairo, Khartoum, Karachi, Buenos Aires, and Sao Paulo. Even in countries that were relatively successful in their adjustment programs, such as Turkey, difficult political pressures arose nine years after adjustment had begun, and wage pressures undermined the ability to achieve fiscal targets. These political risks, usually urban-centered, illustrate the need to assess the urban impacts of adjustment.

The process of urban growth in both the long and short term thus depends heavily on sound macroeconomic management. Fiscal, financial, and monetary stability is necessary to avoid inflation and to allow both public and private investment. Distortions in prices must be corrected to improve efficiency and productivity. The availability of resources to support and expand urban economic activities is heavily conditioned on national fiscal and financial policies and the health of banking systems. Yet, *while sound macroeconomic management is a necessary condition for productive urban growth, it is not a sufficient condition to improve productivity at the city level.* In many countries, national policy change requires a corresponding urban adjustment process to support national economic adjustment. Such a process should result in greater flexibility at the city level to adjust to new macroeconomic realities.

Box 1. Urban Agglomeration Economies

Two kinds of agglomeration economies can be distinguished: localization economies, which are external to the firm but internal to an industry, and urbanization economies, which are external to both the firm and the industry. Localization economies commonly result from the increased demand for goods and services from specific industries. Increased demand leads to increased competition and efficiencies among firms intending to provide inputs to production. The scale of industries itself can thus also generate localization economies. This process extends in many directions, such as through the vertical and horizontal integration of specific industries, where ancillary industries within the same area provide inputs or complementary services to other industries and firms. The growth of enterprises and investment becomes self-reinforcing. This leads to the capture of benefits at the firm and industry level, which further increases the scale of economic activity in specific locations. The growth of cities with concentrations of particular industries, such as textiles in Karachi or financial services in Hong Kong, are examples of localization economies. Even within cities, specific districts may specialize in particular economic activities that take advantage of proximity such as small-scale manufacturing or production and sale of jewelry.

Economies of scale at the firm and industry level also contribute to the emergence of urbanization economies that are external to both firms and industries. They reflect the sum of private and public investments in specific locations, as well as the pools of labor and capital and financial, legal, and public services. Public investment in infrastructure, communications, or environmental services support existing private economic activities and encourage new private investment. Existing and new firms utilize those public investments as part of their own production functions, for example, the use of water supply or electricity in manufacturing. The availability of these inputs in turn adds to the efficiency and increased scale of production and the demand for additional inputs of labor, capital, and technology in specific locations. Public investment "crowds in" private investment. The growth of megacities with large numbers of all kinds of manufacturing and commerce represent, on the positive side, large urbanization economies. The availability of supporting inputs to production reduces the cost and increases industrial efficiency.

The Spatial Dimensions of the Urban Economy

Urban markets benefit from economies of scale and agglomeration and from the proximity of labor, capital, and technology. Cities are the locus of high-density social and economic interactions among individual households and enterprises. The concentration of population and economic activities such as manufacturing, commerce, and banking in specific locations has led to increased demand for goods and services and productivity growth of individual households and enterprises that supply them. The increased scale of production, in turn, results in efficiencies in the uses of labor, capital, technology, and other inputs that result in greater than proportionate increases in output. Economies of scale are most often internal to the firm, while agglomeration economies are external to the firm. Agglomeration economies occur when the concentration of population or economic activity lowers the cost per unit of output or increases the welfare of the population. Agglomeration economies are the benefits of urbanization. (See box 1.)

Investments in one location can result in costs or benefits to others. Positive externalities that result from the combination of economies of scale and agglomeration economies include the increased efficiency resulting from greater access to information, education, and public services such as police and fire protection. Many positive externalities result from spatial proximity and the density of population concentration and economic activity.

In contrast, the negative externalities of concentration include traffic congestion, difficult access in crowded areas, pollution of air and water, and other environmental degradation. These negative externalities reflect the cumulative effect of individual behavior. As cities have grown, public policies and institutions are required to regulate some private behavior and to correct for "market failures." Growing awareness of environmental risks and the weakness of public institutions in managing rapidly expanding urban areas suggests that, from a research perspective, there is a need to revisit the issue of city size and the limits to agglomeration economies in megacities.

Within these spatial dimensions of the urban economy, the challenge of urban policy is to maximize the agglomeration economies and their positive externalities while minimizing the diseconomies and negative externalities. In contrast to the earlier focus of governments and donors, the policy framework presented below focuses on this challenge by reducing the constraints facing urban economic activities through appropriate policies and improving urban institutions. The operational responsibility at the city level belongs to the mayor and local government who must mobilize and manage municipal resources for essential investment and recurrent expenditures for maintaining urban infrastructure and the delivery of urban services. Thus a key task for local government is to enable the full benefits of agglomeration economies to be realized, while managing to reduce negative externalities. The intellectual and practical challenge is to formulate policies that work to reduce the constraints to urban productivity, to alleviate poverty, and to manage the environment in a complementary manner, rather than as tradeoffs.

Reducing the Constraints on the Productivity of the Urban Economy

This section presents the major constraints to improved urban productivity. These include: infrastructure deficiencies, the regulatory framework, weak municipal institutions, and inadequate financial services for urban development. Each imposes significant costs on private-sector activities.

Infrastructure Deficiencies

Urban economic activity depends heavily on infrastructure such as power, roads, and water supply. Similarly, the health of urban populations living in high densities is dependent on sanitation and clean water supplies. Some activities, such as urban transport, are particularly complex because of their effect on settlement patterns and congestion and the high cost often involved. Failures of public management and scarcity of financial and technical capacity have resulted in widespread deficiencies in water supply, electricity, transportation, communications, and solid-waste management. These deficiencies impose heavy burdens on the productive activity of urban households and enterprises. Firms in Lagos, for example, must provide their own electric power. Traffic congestion in Bangkok, Cairo, and Mexico City impede the movement of goods and services and thus reduce the economies of agglomeration of urban markets. Communications are also lacking in many cities: in Sao Paulo there are twice as many cars as telephones. Unreliable sources of water constrain manufacturing processes in Karachi and Lima. Inadequate public collection and disposal of solid waste in many cities add to the deterioration of air, water, and land.

While these phenomena are usually perceived as local problems, they have macroeconomic implications. The *Report on Structural Adjustment Lending II* has emphasized the importance of directing public investment into infrastructure in order to facilitate a timely supply response from the private sector. It noted that even when there is a change of investment incentives, well-targeted public investment in infrastructure may also be necessary to induce private investment. It is ironic that just as countries are beginning to deregulate their industries and liberalize their trade regimes, the infrastructure needed to facilitate this process is crumbling or in urgent need of repair.

The poor condition of infrastructure has been increasingly recognized in different contexts. The effects of a long-term neglect of infrastructure are serious although in some cases they may not be immediately visible. Two of the better performing African economies, Kenya and Malawi, invested in infrastructure in real terms at a rate 30 percent lower than the growth of GNP during 1974-1984. In Tanzania, the reduction in infra-

Box 2.   Infrastructure and Declining Productivity
in the United States

In the United States, total factor productivity growth fell from 2 percent to
0.8 percent per year over the periods 1950-70 to 1971-85. At the same time,
the growth rate of the net stock of nonmilitary public capital dwindled
from 4.1 percent to a mere 1.6 percent per annum. The growth rate of the
public capital stock relative to a "combined" unit of private labor and
capital went from a strongly positive 2.4 percent to a negative 0.6 percent.
    This slowdown in growth, according to one recent study, is explained by
the distribution of government spending on infrastructure. The study
shows that there has been a strong correlation between changes in the level
of total factor productivity and changes in the level of the nonmilitary
public capital stock over the last thirty-five years. It suggests that the
movements in public capital can explain a large portion of the longer term
movements in productivity in the private sector over the period 1949 to
1985. It argues that more than 80 percent of the reduction in productivity
is directly related to the neglect of infrastructure investment.

Source: Aschauer, 1988.

structure investment was much sharper. At the city level, deficiencies in
drinking water, sanitation, and waste disposal are common across the
continent. In Zaire, urban infrastructure services are available to less
than half of the urban population, while public buses are out of service
90 percent of the time. Fewer than 20 percent of attempted telephone calls
are completed. These conditions led the recent World Bank report *Sub-
Saharan Africa: From Crisis to Sustainable Growth* to recommend an increased emphasis on infrastructure as a key ingredient to enable increased
productivity in Africa.
    Infrastructure constraints on urban industry are also serious in in-
dustrializing countries at various levels of income such as Thailand and
Indonesia, and even in an industrialized country such as the United
States. (See box 2.) Urban infrastructure and services are especially
important for industry, because they are intermediate inputs, not only
intended for final consumption, but also essential for producing tradable
goods and services. Where cities are growing rapidly, an inadequate
supply of urban services constrains the growth of productivity of business enterprises and urban households and hence the contribution of
cities to economic development.
    Recent Bank research on urban infrastructure in Nigeria[1] has dem-

---

1.   Lee and Anas (1989).

Box 3. The Cost of Government Regulations to Small Firms

Regulations—frequently imposed by municipal or local governments—
that control the creation and operation of new enterprises are usually
biased against smaller ones. In Lima, Peru, for example, 11 different
permits are required for the establishment of a small textile plant. The cost
of all these permits is equivalent to 32 times the monthly minimum wage
(hereafter read as x minimum wages) and the whole process takes 10
months. Still, it costs—in terms of lost working time, fees. and legal
advice—the equivalent of 15 minimum wages to establish a small store
legally. Since the average street vendor earns about 1.4 minumum wages,
it is virtually impossible for him (or her, since 54 percent of them are
women) to move from informal street vending to legally established small
retailing.

Source: de Soto, 1989.

---

onstrated that unreliable infrastructure services impose heavy costs on
manufacturing enterprises. Virtually every manufacturing firm in Lagos
has its own electric power generator to cope with the unreliable public
power supply. These firms invest 10 to 35 percent of their capital in power
generation alone and incur additional capital and operating expenses to
substitute for other unreliable public services. The burden of investment
in power generation, boreholes, vehicles, and radio equipment in lieu of
working telephones is disproportionately higher for small firms. In
Nigeria and many other low-income countries, manufacturers' high
costs of operation prevent innovation and adoption of new technology
and make it difficult for them to compete in international markets. Cities
with inadequate infrastructure provide a particularly poor environment
for small-scale enterprise. They cannot offer the essential incubator
function for small new entrepreneurs who need to rely on existing
infrastructure and other urban services. [2]

The Regulatory Framework

Urban areas are the centers of most industrial and commercial activities,
but essential markets for goods and services, as well as for urban land and
housing, are often overregulated to the detriment of the urban economy.
The rigidity of regulatory regimes imposed from both the national and
local levels often limits exploiting the productive potential of households
and firms in cities. While some regulations, such as those governing

---

2.   Lee (1985, 1989).

health and safety in housing are desirable, many such as controls on industrial permits impose heavy costs on new enterprises. A typical pattern is one of cumulative regulations imposed over time, each designed to respond to a specific problem. The net effect is to produce higher overall costs that outweigh the intended benefits of individual rules. (See box 3.)

High, unaffordable land use and building standards, often established by national ministries, also constrain local productivity and development. A study of housing markets in Malaysia[3] showed that overly elaborate and time-consuming regulations increased housing costs by up to 50 percent. They imposed an annual cost on the Malaysian economy equivalent to about 3 percent of GDP. More than 50 permits are required to develop a housing area, a costly process that often takes four to seven years. Most of the urban poor are thus shut out from access to land and adequate shelter. By contrast, in the relatively deregulated market in Bangkok, housing costs have actually declined as developers have designed down-market, producing cheaper units at levels of quality acceptable to new owners.

In Colombia, security of tenure in poor urban areas has been essential in motivating household savings for housing improvement.[4] A recent study in the U.K.[5], where housing markets are less distorted than in many countries, demonstrated that rent control inhibited labor mobility and thereby accounted for about half of unemployment. The Urban Land Ceiling and Regulation Act of 1976 in India illustrates how government can exacerbate problems. The Act, which attempted to expropriate vacant urban land for low-income settlement, in effect has taken some thousand square kilometers of vacant land off the market in 73 Indian cities. Partly, as a result, land prices have risen between 10 and 100 percent annually in major Indian cities such as Bombay and Madras. While upward pressures on land prices exist in most cities, normally reflecting the productivity of central city investments, they are accentuated by policies that further reduce supply.

Government regulations tend to have an especially severe impact on the productivity of small enterprises and the poor. The most labor-intensive enterprises, those frequently within the informal sector, are most affected. The costs of regulation tend to be fixed rather than varying with the size of the enterprise, so there is a severe bias against small enterprises. The bias often forces enterprises to operate extralegally.

---

3. World Bank (1989a).

4. Carroll (1981).

5. Gordon (1988); Hughes and McCormick (1988).

Although small urban enterprises avoid some of the heavy costs associated with formal-sector operations (e.g., social security payments), there are other costs such as difficulties in obtaining bank credit and import and other licenses from government. Surveys in low-income urban areas indicate that between 5 and 10 percent of the households are engaged in some kind of home-based manufacturing or retail activity. However, these very types of business activities are frequently prohibited under local zoning regulations.

Regulation is not the sole cause of urban economic distortion. However, countries with highly regulated macroeconomies also tend to have inefficient urban economies. An index[6] measuring economic distortion in a number of developing countries has been plotted against the ratio of house price to income—an indicator of supply constraints in the housing market (see figure 4). As expected, the ratio of house price to income is high in economies with high levels of economic distortion such as Nigeria (before structural adjustment), Egypt, and Turkey, and low in countries such as Thailand where the markets operate more efficiently.

Weak Municipal Institutions

In most countries many essential services in cities are managed by local governments. Public-sector management is commonly a concern at all levels of government but the financial and technical weakness of municipal institutions can place severe constraints on important urban-based economic activities as well as on public health. As noted in Chapter I, the dominant role of national governments in the planning and financing of urban infrastructure in the post-independence period in Asia and Africa has starved local government for financial resources. In no developing country have municipalities had the ability to bid for credit at market rates on a sustainable basis. Yet some municipalities are expected to finance long-term assets without access to finance.

The recent financial crisis has worsened this situation, especially in Latin America where previously well-established municipal institutions have seriously declined in the absence of central government transfers and with simultaneous disruptions in financial markets. Central control of financial resources has limited local financial autonomy and efforts to mobilize resources. In many countries, central governments assign narrow-based or politically controversial tax bases to local authorities

---

6. Agarwala (1983) constructed an index of distortions as a measure of the policy environment including distortions in exchange rates, interest rates, agricultural prices, wages, protection rates for manufacturing, general price level, and infrastructure pricing, for 31 developing countries.

Figure 4. House Price to Income Ratio and Level of Distortions

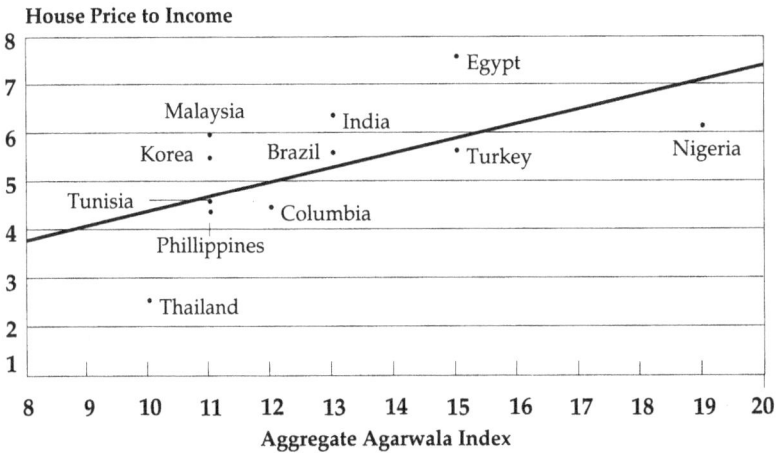

and then further constrain local resource mobilization by controlling the rates of local taxation. Intergovernmental transfers, which account for more than half of local recurrent revenue, give perverse incentives: recurrent transfers frequently reward local governments with the largest deficits. They also substitute transfers for the financial intermediation that might occur if municipalities could issue debt.

The results of this situation are reflected in a 1984 survey of 86 developing countries which found that property taxes averaged less than 1 percent of total revenue. Insufficient local revenues have often resulted in an overreliance on central government transfers or large operating deficits with serious macroeconomic consequences. A review of government finances during 1978-86 in 19 countries concluded that the deficits of subnational governments (provincial and municipal) accounted for an average of 50 percent of the consolidated government deficit. In Argentina the deficit of subnational governments (provincial and municipal) amounted to 6 percent of GDP. The impact of the financial weakness of local government thus goes beyond urban areas, and it affects macro-fiscal performance. Consequently, addressing central-local financial relations is necessary both to ensure a stable but buoyant local financial base and to protect macroeconomic balances.

It is clear that municipalities require access to sufficient buoyant sources of revenue to provide local services. Most local governments have local revenue sources, commonly the property tax and some local business taxation, but local sources typically account for less than half of total revenue. Improvement in tax assessment and collection can increase revenues over the long term, but additional sources are frequently necessary to meet short-term needs. Centrally controlled revenue-sharing programs are usually managed arbitrarily. If local governments are to achieve meaningful autonomy, they require access to credit so they can finance major capital investments. Since some form of revenue sharing and capital lending is used in most countries, the terms of these transfers should be conducive to effective resource use. Consumers of urban infrastructure and services financed with these funds should understand the costs involved. The pricing of infrastructure and services, therefore, should include meeting their capital and recurrent costs.

Financial considerations lead to the importance of strengthening the technical capacity of municipal institutions as well. The ambiguity of central-local responsibilities often reduces local accountability and the efficiency of service delivery. For example, responsibilities for important local services, such as water supply and sewerage, are often retained by central government agencies. These state monopolies can be a means of consolidating scarce technical skills, but they can also lead to unclear responsibilities at the local level. Where central agencies design and construct infrastructure and turn it over to local authorities, poor operation and maintenance often follows. Many regulations such as pollution and land-use control are made at the central level and are expected to be enforced locally. Problems of local responsibility can be compounded when local governments report to central ministries, which must approve municipalities' budgets and tax rates and other operations. That often makes them more accountable to the central government than to their own citizens. The problem is exacerbated because the local government ministries themselves are inefficient, lacking information or expertise for decisionmaking.

The internal organization of local government also often leads to serious inefficiency. Mayors typically centralize responsibility with little delegation of decisionmaking to service departments. Another common problem is management through large, indecisive committees. Professional staff often lack adequate skills and motivation, owing in part to poor career opportunities. Excessive staffing permeates at lower levels. Accounting systems tend not to generate adequate management information. The budgeting process often overestimates revenue, leading to unrealistic revenue projections and work programs.

Inadequate Financial Services

A poorly developed financial sector poses major constraints to urban investment, both public infrastructure investment and private investment in the housing stock. Housing typically accounts for 2 to 8 percent of GDP and 15 to 30 percent of fixed capital formation. Weak and undeveloped

Box 4. The U.S. Savings and Loan Crisis

The crisis of the United States saving and loan associations (S&Ls) is a well-known, but not unusual, example of the problems of financing urban investments. This crisis shows how things can go wrong, and, more important, how much it can cost.

The difficulties of the S&Ls began in the late 1970s. They had traditionally lent funds on 20- to 30-year mortgages at fixed interest rates and funded themselves with short-term deposits. Higher inflation rates in the late 1970s and early 1980s and the correspondingly higher interest rates that S&Ls had to pay on deposits sharply depressed earnings. As part of the process of financial deregulation, the interest rate ceilings on deposits were phased out, new lending practices were allowed, and the maximum size of an insured deposit went up from US$40,000 to US$100,000. Unfortunately, policy-makers paid less attention to strengthening the system of prudential regulation and supervision of the net worth of the institutions.

The increased lending powers gave S&Ls new opportunities for loss as well as profit. Moreover, as firms, they were required to risk little of their own capital: any losses beyond the low levels of capital in the firms were to be absorbed by the U.S. government. This kind of financial structure ensured a plentiful supply of mortgage credit and competitive mortgage lenders. Unfortunately, it also induced much greater risk-taking by the S&Ls. In the event that this risk-taking imposed losses on the U.S. government, the present value of the loss is likely to exceed US$150 billion, which is a tax equivalent to about US$2,000 for every family in the country.

The lessons learned from the U.S. experience are by no means unique. Indeed, when the U.S. experience is compared with the experiences of developing countries in recent years, an important lesson emerges: the policies designed to ensure that urban and housing finance is available often lie at the center of the difficulties in deregulating financial systems. For example, following deregulation in Colombia, the forced investments of the banking system, overwhelmingly in low interest rate housing bonds, played an important part in the financial distress experienced by these lenders; in Brazil, the role of BHN, the housing and infrastructure bank, in the financial disruptions of the early 1980s is well known; and finally, in Mexico, the costs to the banking system of the forced mortgage lending, prior to a Bank project, was estimated at US$400 million a year.

While financial deregulation is likely to continue as developing countries place increasing emphasis on domestic resource mobilization, it will also continue to be constrained by the need to develop sustainable and non-inflationary housing finance systems.

financial systems that are unable to mobilize private savings have led governments to adopt housing finance policies dependent on public resources. Public-housing finance schemes have frequently involved large subsidies, financed implicitly either by savers or by governments themselves. Many low-income households and small enterprises are denied access to credit because of lack of collateral or by other legal or institutional constraints. This constrains urban investment. It creates additional pressure for central government expenditure to finance high-return investments that households and local governments could finance if they had access to credit markets.

The links between the financial sector and the urban economy do not run in one direction. Pressure for financial subsidies for the urban sector, especially in middle-income countries with more highly developed urban financial systems, has frequently retarded the development of financial systems at the national level. It has contributed to budget deficits, high inflation, and a much less competitive financial system.[7] Denying households and local governments access to credit at market rates, as in most developed countries, places a severe limit on the demand for, and cost of, credit. In the U.S. during the 1970s, state and local governments and households together accounted for more than 40 percent of outstanding debt of nonfinancial borrowers—a greater share than the corporate sector.[8] Credit subsidies for housing in Argentina and Pakistan exceed direct housing subsidies made by government. The combination of inflation and a lack of appropriate mortgage instruments has led to the rapid decapitalization and financial failure of housing finance institutions in many developing countries, as in the case of the Housing Bank of Brazil. The crisis of the savings and loan associations in the United States illustrates that the contingent liabilities created by local financial institutions for national governments can easily become real losses in an ineffective regulatory environment. (See box 4.) This urban-macro-financial link is also evident in Hungary, where the National Housing Bank is the largest and most insolvent bank in the country. Thus the reform of urban-related finance, particularly of housing, should play a major role in the adjustment process and constitute a key part of financial sector reform. It does not involve establishing new forms of directed credit through public institutions, but rather establishing a "level playing field" in which the financial needs of urban investment can compete with the demand for financing other investments in the economy.

Alleviating Urban Poverty

The challenge of urban management in the economic environment of the 1990s is how to improve productivity while directly alleviating the growing incidence of urban poverty and thereby also improving equity. This does not require a trade-off between strategies to promote economic

---

7. Buckley and Mayo (1989).
8. Friedman (1980).

growth and to reduce poverty; poverty reduction is possible in part through improving productivity at the individual, household, firm, and urban levels. This approach involves both directly increasing the labor intensity of productive investment and improving the human capital of the poor through better education, health, and nutrition.

While data are not available to determine the effects of adjustment on the urban income distribution, it is nonetheless evident that the relatively higher incomes of the middle class have been reduced in real terms by reduced subsidies of which they had been the major beneficiaries. This has also affected lower middle-class groups for whom these subsidies constituted a significant part of their real incomes. The process has pushed them into the lower income category, at least until the resumption of growth leads to improved opportunities for employment, higher productivity, and increased wages. These consequences have been a necessary part of the process of returning to sustainable economic balances and improving overall equity between the urban and rural populations.

If the decline in urban real incomes resulting from adjustment policies is in fact a transitional problem, a larger problem remains. It is that of increasing numbers of urban poor due to demographic growth and constraints on urban productivity. As has been noted, Bank estimates indicate that the urban poor account for about 25 percent of the total urban population—some 330 million people in 1988. While many causes of urban poverty can be traced to structural constraints and inefficiencies in the urban economy (including excessive protection of capital-intensive industry, ineffective public policies, and weak public institutions) the condition of the urban poor is affected by macroeconomic developments as well.

Lahore, Pakistan. Overcrowding forces the urban poor to live outside.

By the late 1980s, urban per capita incomes in some countries had reverted to 1970 levels and in some cases to 1960 levels (Madagascar, Zaire). In Poland and Yugoslavia urban poverty grew much faster than rural poverty during the period from 1978 to 1987, owing in part to a change in the terms of trade between the rural and urban economies and the opening of market opportunities in rural areas. (See figure 5.) In some countries, such as Ghana and Nigeria, increases in urban poverty were aggravated by collapses of the formal urban labor market. The poorest households are most frequently those headed by women, with the least assets, the most dependents, and particularly severe constraints on time.

In addition to decreases in urban real wages, investment has been reduced. Together with a shifting demand for labor, that has resulted in increasing unemployment and larger numbers of day laborers rather than long-term employed workers. The link between reduced investment and unemployment is most evident in construction, which traditionally absorbs large amounts of unskilled labor. Three broad channels link adjustment to the incidence of poverty:

- *Wages.* Since the urban poor are especially dependent on their labor, rather than asset ownership, they bear the greatest risk when unemployment rises. Restrictive monetary and fiscal policies affect the urban poor through contractions in urban labor markets.

Figure 5. Rural and Urban Poverty, 1978–1987

Poverty Rates

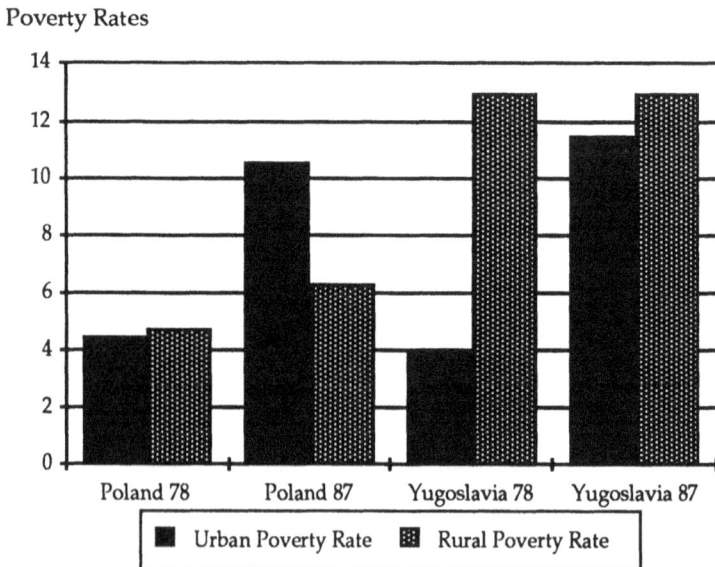

- *Prices.* Wages adjust much more slowly than the prices of goods and services as adjustment reduces absorption and as currency devaluations impose upward pressure on import prices. Whereas the rural poor might derive some benefit from exchange devaluation, the urban poor are net losers. In addition, fiscal reform usually involves real increases in tariffs, which again tend to affect the urban poor disproportionately.
- *Public Services.* Cuts in public expenditure are usually a necessary component of adjustment programs, including reductions in public health or education as well as infrastructure investment, which tend to be disproportionately important to the poor.

These links between macroeconomic developments and impacts on the urban poor are important on both equity and efficiency grounds. Despite the design of safety-net programs to mitigate these effects, many individual households are poorer because of the macroeconomic crisis. Whether this situation will improve depends on the extent to which the productive contribution of the urban poor to the urban economy is recognized and supported. This will require an appropriate strategy to stimulate the demand for labor while ensuring, through provision of adequate social services and infrastructure, that the poor can take advantage of the opportunities provided.

World Development Report 1990 confirms that

> rapid and politically sustainable progress on poverty has been achieved by pursuing a strategy that has two equally important elements. The first is to promote the productive use of the poor's most abundant asset—labor. It calls for policies that harness market incentives, social and political institutions, infrastructure, and technology to that end. The second is to provide basic social services to the poor. Primary health care, family planning, nutrition, and primary education are especially important.

This strategy is consistent with the overall policy framework developed in this paper, a framework that aims at enhancing the productivity of urban households and enterprises accompanied by better access to urban services.

In most cities in developing countries, large proportions of total population live in informal settlements where structural problems exist concerning the access of the poor to essential services. Rigid regulatory regimes and deficient infrastructure have historically had their worst impacts on the poor. Regulations often give the poor no alternative to informal settlements and limit access to basic services. Water-supply systems in these areas are usually rudimentary. Many low-income households buy water from vendors, paying 10 percent or more of their income for a few gallons of water a day. In Cali, Colombia, the urban poor

---

Box 5. The High Cost of Being Poor

In many cases, policies that are focused to reduce the prices of urban necessities by improving infrastructure provision and revising regulatory frameworks should be seen as an essential complement to any policies designed to raise the incomes of the poor. An influential and pathbreaking book in the 1960s, *The Poor Pay More* (Caplovitz, 1967), captured in its title one of the fundamental realities of not the low-income New York community, but of thousands of other urban communities around the world. The study documented that for what the poor got, they paid higher prices for food, shelter, furniture, clothing, and credit than did their better-off contemporaries in New York City, increasing their economic vulnerability and decreasing their self-reliance.

The same phenomenon exists in the cities of the developing world, but with even more severe consequences for the poor than in developed countries. Food costs, for example, are considerably more for urban than for rural populations, with the result that food consumption is frequently inadequate among the urban poor. In Tunisia, the cost per calorie of food intake among households in small cities with below average incomes was 22 percent higher than the cost among rural households; among below average income households in large cities, the cost per calorie was 37 percent higher than that of comparable rural households. Among the two lowest income groups studied, however, the relative costs of food were still higher—33 percent and 55 percent higher than the costs confronted by rural populations with similar incomes. These large differences in food prices are only partly offset by a food subsidy scheme, which, despite having become a significant burden on the national budget, is equivalent

---

buy water of substandard quality from inefficient private vendors at prices 10 times higher than could be provided by public authorities. In Guayaquil, Ecuador, drinking water supplied by tank to slum areas costs 20 times as much as if it were piped. (See box 5.) Similar situations have been documented for African countries. [9] These deficiencies lead to health problems, including malnutrition and diarrheal and other waterborne diseases. (See box 6.) The lack of even basic social services in many settlements has resulted in local-level initiatives and the increasing involvement of community-level organizations and nongovernmental organizations in the delivery and maintenance of social services.

The *World Development Report* also confirms that the informal sector "plays a prominent role in providing employment and incomes. It has been estimated to account for 75 percent of urban employment in many countries in Sub-Saharan Africa and for 85 percent in Pakistan." Despite the important contribution of the urban informal sector to urban economic

---

9. Whittington, Lauria, and Mu (1989).

only to about 7 percent of the incomes of the poor in Tunisian cities. As a result, low-income consumers are extremely vulnerable to increases in the price of cereal products, which made up the bulk of their diets, and they are far more likely than their rural counterparts to suffer from malnutrition.

Housing costs are another significant burden for the urban poor. Studies of housing consumption patterns in developing countries have found that the poor almost inevitably pay higher fractions of their incomes for housing than do better-off households. In poorer countries, the poor may pay 10 percent of their incomes for housing while households with average incomes pay only 6-7 percent. In better-off developing countries, the poor may spend as much as 30-40 percent of their incomes for rent while average income households spend only 20 percent of income (Mayo, Malpezzi, and Gross, 1986). In many cases, the high housing prices in developing countries are brought about in part by inappropriate government interventions in housing and land markets, which often have relatively more severe deleterious impacts on the poor than on better-off households.

Another major element in consumer budgets in developing country cities is water. Failure of authorities to provide adequate access to water results in poor urban households having to buy small amounts of water, often at exorbitant prices, from water vendors. In the Klong Toey slum in Bangkok, the cost per month of water was equivalent to four days wages. And in Nouakchott, Mauritiana, "frequently water has to be bought from a water merchant, with no guarantee as to quality and with the price up to 100 times that paid by those with piped water connections." (Harpham et at, 1988).

High prices for these and other necessities place at risk the very existence of substantial fractions of the urban poor in developing countries.

---

activity, striving entrepreneurs in the informal sector in developing countries are severely constrained from expanding their enterprises and generating more employment. Rigid regulatory mechanisms; deficit infrastructure such as electricity, water, and transport; and prohibitive credit requirements all unnecessarily limit the productive potential of this sector. As is discussed in the next chapter, governments can provide greater incentives for informal activities by changing regulations and providing adequate infrastructure services to increase the productivity of these entrepreneurs. (See box 14.)

The Urban Environment

One of the major consequences of constrained urban productivity and increasing urban poverty is the deterioration of the urban environment in developing countries. Urban environmental problems such as air and water pollution are exacerbated by urban densities and congestion. They are prime examples of the negative externalities discussed earlier. They have become increasingly visible, with serious implications for public health and for the long-term viability of the urban economy. Especially in megacities, the seeming intractability of the immense problems of air and water pollution and water-resource depletion is drawing worldwide attention. Thus, in addition to the special problem of urban poverty, urban environmental issues deserve to be included as an integral part of the urban policy framework.

Environmental Problems in Cities

Some types of urban environmental problems have their most detrimental impact on human health. In poorer developing countries, waterborne bacteria are the most serious cause of disease. In more developed countries, air pollution associated with higher incomes and vehicular transport become more significant. In 1987 less than 60 percent of the urban population had access to adequate sanitation, and only one-third was connected to sewer systems.[10] Where sewerage did exist, 90 percent of the wastewater was discharged without treatment. Thus most human excreta remained in the residential environment or was discharged nearby. As cities continue to grow, these problems also grow.

Collection and disposal of household garbage is a persistent problem in most cities. Typically less than half the urban population has its garbage collected. Collection is especially poor in lower income areas, where trucks have difficult access.

Air pollution is becoming a growing problem, particularly in cities in middle-income countries. Data from the WHO/UNEP Global Environmental Monitoring System indicate that 20 of 23 participating developing country cities do not meet WHO guidelines for suspended particulate matter and sulfur dioxide emissions.[11] In many cities, conditions are worsening as emissions from fuel use and industry increase. Vehicle fleets and emissions are expected to grow 5 to 10 percent a year in developing countries.[12] Indoor air pollution, mainly from the use of traditional fuels for cooking and heating, is also a serious problem.

Impacts of Environmental Degradation

The main health risks from environmental degradation come from pathogens in the environment, indoor air pollution and substandard

---

10. World Health Organization (1987).

11. Global Environmental Monitoring System (1987).

12. OECD (1988).

Box 6. Health and Nutrition Among the Poor
in Third World Countries

From a recent review of descriptive and analytic studies in urban areas of industrialized and developing countries, it seems that the health impact of both chronic and acute morbidity and consequent mortality is upon the urban poor. Urban poverty is a complex proxy measure for a composite of deprivation extending from control over resources, education, social support, and self-esteem to environmental factors such as housing quality and access to water and sanitation services. But as a fundamental variable, poverty remains the most significant predictor of urban morbidity and mortality.

The urban poor in developing countries suffer the "worst of both worlds." They experience the problems of underdeveloped populations (deaths from infectious diseases and a predominance of post-natal over neonatal deaths) and the problems of industrialized populations (deaths from neoplasms, heart disease, and accidents). The following facts emerge from the studies reviewed:

- In contrast to higher income urbanites and oftentimes rural populations, the urban poor have lower life expectancy at birth and higher infant mortality.
- The relationship of infant and child mortality with quality and access to water and sanitation is significant—children from households using public standposts or cess pits are three to five times more likely to die of diarrhea than those with in house piped water and sewerage.
- Urban poor households often have much worse nutritional status than rural households.
- Female children in slums are further disadvantaged compared with males in terms of differential nutrition, health care, and mortality.
- When a child from a slum is old enough to independently move about the city, he or she becomes increasingly exposed to death associated with motor accidents (five to fourteen years) and homicides (fifteen to nineteen years).
- In youth and early adults, mortality differentials may be due to communicable disease and violence in males, and in females rather less from violence and more from obstetric causes.
- From fifteen years onward, trauma and chronic diseases play a substantial role in mortality and morbidity—one particular problem being occupational exposure in small-scale and cottage industry and exposure in the home.
- Communicable disease is likely to reappear as a major cause of intraurban differentials in the elderly.

(WHO, 1988; Harpham et al, 1988).

housing, and industrialization. Mortality and morbidity from gastroenteric and respiratory diseases are linked to substandard housing and services. Diarrhea and respiratory infections are leading killers of infants in the less developed countries. Acute respiratory infections in children and chronic bronchitis in women stem from inadequate housing and especially smoke exposure. Air pollution and exposure to toxic chemicals also exact a heavy health toll. For instance, in 1980 in the heavily polluted industrial city of Cubatao, Brazil, forty out of every one thousand babies were stillborn, and forty more died in the first week of life. Subsequent improvements in air quality have led to better health conditions. [13]

Environmental degradation can also have long-term effects on resources, threatening not only human health and ecosystems, but also sustainability of development. Groundwater depletion or contamination can be serious. The loss of land resources poses another serious problem when, for example, development of erosion-prone areas, coastal zones, or wetlands is not controlled. Hazardous industrial wastes cause particular concern, since it is difficult to monitor discharges and ensure that they are not put into sewers or landfills. The sophisticated facilities needed to treat and dispose of hazardous wastes do not exist in most developing countries. Many countries have dangerous backlogs of hazardous waste requiring treatment and disposal that threaten land or groundwater resources. Many environmental problems with national and international implications, such as carbon dioxide, sulphur dioxide, and nitrous oxide emissions have their origin in urban industry and transport.

Determinants of Urban Environmental Degradation

Assessment of the underlying causes of urban environmental problems is the important first step in designing strategies to address them. Some causes, such as rapid population growth are fundamental. Others involve inadequate preventive action through economic policy and management measures such as (i) inappropriate economic policies (e.g., underpricing of water and other services), leading to resource depletion and higher levels of pollution and (ii) inadequate land use control or inappropriate land tenure systems that hinder effective land use or lead to overregulation of land markets and force the poor to occupy marginal lands. Other causes stem from inadequate curative actions such as (a) use of inappropriate technologies (e.g., waterborne sanitation when less costly on-site disposal systems would be feasible), (b) inadequate investment in pollution control, and (c) insufficient enforcement of environ-

---

13.   Briscoe (1989).

mental regulations. Insufficient political will is a common problem, particularly when environmental degradation is far away or delayed or when traditions of public environmental awareness and action have not yet developed.

This chapter has presented a policy framework for improving the contribution of cities to economic growth. It has distinguished between national and city-level policies and sought to identify policy reform, institutional development, and investments that are possible at the city level and applicable to regional cities of varying sizes as well as the primate city. These actions fit within a broader perspective of urban management within the spatial dimensions of the urban economy. The challenge of urban policy is, in abstract terms, how to maximize the agglomeration economies and their positive externalities while minimizing the diseconomies and negative externalities. The operational challenge is to formulate policies and actions that address the three central problems of urban growth: reducing the constraints to urban productivity, alleviating poverty, and managing the environment in a complementary manner, rather than as trade-offs. The stakes involved in urban policy reform are large. Indeed, they are of national dimensions. However, the policy analysis and institutional change required to bring about change are likely to be time-consuming and costly. They will require a commitment by the countries themselves as well as by the international community.

3

The New Urban Agenda for the 1990s:
A Strategy for the Developing Countries

The growing interdependence between the urban economy and macroeconomic performance requires *a new urban agenda for the developing countries and the international community in the 1990s* and beyond. The legacy of inadequate government response and the limited impact of donor assistance requires a change in objectives for urban policy.

First, it is of paramount importance to ensure the productivity of the urban economy and its contribution to macroeconomic performance by reducing the constraints to urban productivity. This requires—

- Strengthening the management of urban infrastructure at the city level, to include improving the level and composition of investment and reinforcing institutional capacity for operations and maintenance.
- Improving the citywide regulatory framework to increase market efficiency and to enhance the role of the private sector in shelter and infrastructure provision.
- Improving the financial and technical capacity of municipal institutions through more effective division of resources and responsibilities between central and local governments.
- Strengthening financial services for urban development.

Second, it is critical to increase the contribution of the urban poor to the urban economy while directly alleviating the growing incidence of urban poverty. This requires addressing—
The economic aspects of poverty, through—

- Increasing the demand for the labor of the poor through government support for labor-intensive productive activities.
- Alleviating the structural constraints inhibiting the productivity and growth of the informal sector by reforming regulations and codes that limit the access of the poor to urban services, infrastructure, credit, and markets.
- Increasing the labor productivity of the poor by reducing con-

54

straints preventing labor-force participation, such as constraints on women's time, such as childcare and other responsibilities.

The social aspects of poverty, through—

- Increasing social-sector expenditure for human-resource development of the urban poor by providing basic services in education, health, nutrition, family planning, and vocational training.
- Increasing the access of the poor to infrastructure and housing to meet their basic needs.
- Recognizing and supporting the efforts of the poor to meet their own needs through community initiatives and local, nongovernmental organizations.

Targeted "safety net" assistance to those most vulnerable to short-term shocks, such as children and women who head households, through—

- Direct transfers in food assistance, health care, employment, and provision of other basic needs on a short-term basis.
- Measures to moderate the decline in private consumption.

Third, there is a need to develop sustainable approaches to the management of the urban environment. This requires—

- Raising global awareness of the urban environmental crisis, in order to develop the political support for action.
- Improving the information base and understanding of the dynamics of environmental deterioration in urban areas.
- Developing city-specific urban environmental strategies that respond to the circumstances of individual cities.
- Identifying programs of curative action at the city level to redress the most serious environmental consequences of past public policies and private behavior.
- Formulating effective national and urban policies and incentives to prevent further environmental deterioration.

Fourth, there is a need to increase the level and broaden the scope of research and development in the urban sector. Improving understanding of new patterns of urban growth, such as the emergence of megacities or the urban linkages to macroeconomic performance, is essential to strengthening policy formulation at the international, national, and local levels. In view of the diversity of local conditions and capacities to respond, there is a need to develop a broad-based learning approach. This requires—

- Assessing current urban research in the developing and developed countries in light of the issues raised in this paper.
- Formulating a broad, long-term urban research strategy with national and local research institutions.

- Mobilizing resources to support the expansion of research capacity, particularly in the developing countries.

Agenda Item I: Improving Urban Productivity

Strengthen the Management of Urban Infrastructure

Chapters I and II have highlighted the costs of infrastructure deficiencies. Addressing these problems requires strengthening the management of urban infrastructure. In the past, this has been pursued through individual projects in neighborhoods or for specific categories of citywide infrastructure. In the context of the spatial extension of cities in the 1990s, strengthened management of infrastructure should be undertaken on a citywide level (see box 7). This would include (i) increasing the level of infrastructure investment in some countries; (ii) improving the composition of investment—for example, ensuring the balance between primary networks and neighborhood distribution systems; (iii) improving the operational performance of investments; and (iv) improving the maintenance and rehabilitation of existing investments. This also means improving institutional performance. In some regions—as in Africa, for one—the "infrastructure crisis," will require acting on all four fronts simultaneously. In other regions, such as Latin America, the problem of

---

Box 7. Curitiba, Brazil: Coordinated Management through Information Systems

Curitiba, with a metropolitan region population in 1990 of 2.6 million, is noted for its success in handling urban growth. This occurred with the help of guided development—closely coordinated transport operations linked with new settlement development. In support of this process, it has implemented and enforced zoning regulations and building controls. To facilitate development and land subdivision approvals, it has established building and land information systems to monitor growth and to support rapid approval decision making: a development application takes just five days to process. The municipality of Curitiba, population 1.6 million within the metropolitan region, has established an agency for planning and research—Espaco Urbano—Pesquisa e Planejamento (IPPUC)—responsible also for coordination, priority setting for public work, and information provision. IPPUC coordinates the municipal and infrastructure agencies through infrastructure investment, multiprogram reviews, and a metropolitan financial information system. It has also channeled federal government subsidies for low-income earners into its guided development programs (e.g., bus fares and food programs for new settlement areas).

maintenance is more critical. Substantial new investment may not be needed if existing assets are operated and maintained efficiently. In most cities, however, *maintenance itself has become a development priority.* This means that recent increased efforts to improve the capacity of city governments (and in some cases state-owned enterprises) and to maintain existing infrastructure networks, facilities, and services should be continued and strengthened as a priority objective.

Donor efforts to support governments in municipal management and infrastructure maintenance are well justified in all regions. Intensified programs in African cities are clearly high-priority efforts. Similar activities in cities and towns in other countries are needed to avoid the heavy costs of infrastructure deterioration that have already been identified in the deterioration of interurban road networks. Programs to rehabilitate urban water-supply systems are critical if cities are to receive the full stream of benefits from these past investments.

Improve the Regulatory Framework to Increase Market Efficiency and Private Sector Participation

Changing the citywide regulatory framework governing markets for land and housing in urban areas presents one of the most pressing targets for policy reform. Regulatory reform should play a key role in expanding supply and lowering costs of housing, finance, infrastructure, and developable land and increasing business opportunities. In the past, changing regulations has often occurred at the project level, through exceptions to existing rules. The most common example is waivers on building codes for projects financed with external funds. This approach has had limited impact. It does not affect the city as a whole and, in some cases, after projects are completed, the waiver lapses for the project areas themselves. This limited perspective should be replaced by a citywide approach to regulation. Two techniques should be utilized in developing a reform strategy. First, market assessments should be undertaken. They would identify patterns of supply, demand, and constraints to supply. Assessments of land markets in Bangkok, Karachi, Jakarta, and Tianjin have demonstrated the significance of this analysis in formulating more effective regulatory policy (see box 9). Second, regulatory audits should be carried out to assess the costs, benefits, and distributional consequences of specific regulations at the city level.

These exercises should provide an understanding of the objectives of regulatory reform. The next step would be to formulate regulatory reform programs, devoting particular attention to the impact of different choices of either national or local instruments to be used. These include, in the case of land—

Box 8. Regulatory Reform in Mexico City

Prior to the September 1985 earthquake in Mexico City, a severe shortage in housing existed owing to the tight regulatory environment that included binding rent control for over forty years. In this environment, landlords had no incentive to maintain their buildings, which they subdivided extensively. Such sub-division not only further reduced the already low level of services provided by the housing, but it also made the housing even more vulnerable to earthquake damage. Unfortunately, it took a major disaster to bring about policy change to reform this regulatory environment. The earthquake's widespread damage and destruction of housing in seventy low-income barrios called for immediate and effective results from the government. The immediacy of the need required that the regulatory straitjacket be loosened.

   With the help of the Bank, the government relaxed regulations to land acquisition and ownership and housing loans, allowed small firms to construct new stock and rehabilitate damaged stock with little up-front capital, and relied heavily on existing institutional arrangements to respond. Today, families own and reside in condominiums on the same site where they once rented one small room. The success of this experience provides lessons concerning planning, design, management, and administration of projects both for urban housing and disaster reconstruction programs. Perhaps more important, it demonstrates that strict regulations on rent, land, and finance can often hurt those it was intended to help.

- Fiscal and monetary instruments such as tax incentives, capital gains taxes, land transfer taxes, property taxes, betterment levies, and targeted subsidies.
- Legal instruments such as land-use controls, land tenure, accepted practices and procedures for contractual law, land registration, land allocation, flexible mortgage instruments, and procedures for public acquisition.
- Institutional measures to facilitate transactions in land markets such as land valuation systems and information systems to monitor land ownership patterns, prices, and transfers.

The process of regulatory reform should also lead to an assessment of whether it is preferable not to rely on improvements in public sector performance or to examine the possibilities for private sector provision of services. The challenge is to find medium-term policy options that compromise between two extreme cases of inefficiency of the nonperforming public sector and costly private service provision by individual firms and households. Minor regulatory changes can generate significant benefits to firms and households. For example, Nigerian

Box 9. Land Market Assessments

Knowledge about the operation of land markets in terms of prices, supply of land, plots and housing by location, and type of units provides a needed foundation for defining appropriate strategies for improving market performance and urban development. Assessments should be used in the preparation of urban projects to try to improve the overall delivery processes of urban land for all urban purposes. This is particularly important for low- and moderate-income housing; it requires investigating the major elements blocking improved supply: lack of land, infrastructure, and finance. Land market assessments address questions, such as: what is the demand for land and housing by distinct market segments? What are the present and likely future roles of the public and private sectors, and both the formal and informal land developers? What legal, regulatory, institutional, and procedural changes would streamline the supply processes?

Major empirical studies have been undertaken in Bogota, Bangkok, Karachi, Tianjin, and most recently in Jakarta. The 1988 study in Jakarta found price increases above the initial price of land amounted to between 10 and 29 percent and could be attributed to delayed approvals and legal subdivision processes, sometimes taking up to three years. The Karachi study showed that the public housing authority was subsidizing land plot purchase by discounting them between 30 and 50 percent of the market price with no positive social outcome. The same agency was critically short of capital to finance infrastructure and could not address the needs of low-income earners.

The outcome of these studies has intensified policy dialogues with governments to address the major issues during subsequent project preparation. The Bangkok study assisted the government in its determination to facilitate the private sector in middle- and low-income housing provision and its resolve for housing the poor through its national housing authority. In Indonesia the study contributed to the formulation of a housing policy and strategy. In Karachi the assessment contributed to a policy dialogue in drawing-up proposals for the major national low-income shelter project that was under preparation in 1990.

Based on: Dowall, 1988.

manufacturers are not allowed to sell the excess power they produce to the public agency or to other firms. The potential savings from allowing such transactions can be large. Allowing private vendors to produce and sell electric power (and other services such as transport, water supply, and waste disposal) could provide useful competition to public sector agencies.

A sensible complement to regulatory reform would thus be to encourage private sector participation in infrastructure-related activities. Indeed, in Nigeria, Côte d'Ivoire, and many other countries, private firms are already engaged in the management of infrastructure-related activities such as maintenance and distribution of water supply or billing and collection. In Brazil urban transport is the launch-pad for experimental partnerships in which private firms are given management contracts for joint public-private investments. A Bank-assisted project in Guinea includes training of small construction enterprises.

The challenge is to create appropriate incentive systems for private entrepreneurs to supply infrastructure services, through either production, distribution, maintenance, administration, metering and monitoring, or bill collection. The feasibility of creating and expanding such markets for the supply of these services by the private sector lies in the fact that the users are willing to pay for more reliable services when they are available.[14] To the extent that the markets for certain infrastructure services are contestable because there are no large sunk costs in capital facilities, it should be feasible to ease restrictions—through deregulation—against private entrepreneurs. Under this new environment, the role of the government would be limited to monitoring and supervising these more efficient private operations. Positive experiences in private solid waste collection and disposal in Brazil, management of urban water supply in Chile, and power generation in several countries suggests that private sector provision of infrastructure services can be positive if the regulatory framework is well defined and enforced. Other, more ambitious proposals deserve greater attention. These include such vehicles as private sector financing of major infrastructure projects such as the elevated highway and rapid transit system in Bangkok and build-operate-transfer schemes for infrastructure investment. It should be noted, though, that the practical difficulties of launching these operations are considerable.

Improve the Financial and Technical Capacity of Municipal Institutions

Pursuing a strategy of less centralized urban management offers the possibility of achieving more efficient public service provision. The challenge is to strengthen municipal institutions in a manner that mutually reinforces financial and technical capacity and establishes productive linkages between central government and municipal authorities. In contrast to past government and donor efforts that have focused largely on municipal institutions themselves, responding to this challenge re-

---

14.   Lee and Anas (1989); Whittington, Lauria, and Mu (1989).

quires redefining the conditions and process of central-local interactions as a prior step to enable municipal strengthening to be successful.

Efforts to improve municipal capacity must therefore address several issues:

- The division of central and local functional responsibilities must be mandated in relation to a realistic assessment of local capacities. Colombia, for example, is committed to decentralizing responsibility for water supply, sanitation, urban transport, and primary education to local governments by 1992, yet rapid fiscal decentralization at the end of the 1980s has not been accompanied by strengthening technical capacity at the local level.
- Reallocation of some responsibilities requires that local government be given the authority and autonomy needed to respond to local priorities. Local government should have access to buoyant, politically acceptable sources of revenue and the power to exploit these tax bases effectively through local control over tax rates. It also requires an increase in autonomy over expenditure, both in the allocation of the recurrent budget and in the selection of investment projects.
- Corresponding improvements in organization and management are also needed within local government. Local government management practices tend to be overly centralized. The municipal executive is often preoccupied with the minutiae of day-to-day operations to the neglect of overall strategy and policy direction.
- Local governments need stronger financial management. Budgets

---

Box 10. Local Government Development: Training and Technical Assistance in Calcutta

In May 1982, the Government of West Bengal recognized that local government staff needed more systematic training in supervisory, managerial, and other technical skills and established the Institute of Local Government and Urban Studies (ILGUS). With support from the World Bank in the Third Calcutta Urban Development Project, the Institute aimed at directly training 10,000 persons over a five-year period. Its courses include municipal management, role of state government in municipal administration, comparative municipal administration, low-cost sanitation, municipal resource mobilization, and specialized topics, such as property assessment. The institute publishes a newsletter to disseminate information about municipal and urban administration. It also consults municipal bodies on their managerial problems. As of 1990 the institute is continuing to train local government personnel throughout the Calcutta Metropolitan Area and to conduct urban research.

must be realistic tools for priority setting. Financial reporting must be timely to be useful in policy making. The format of accounts must identify the costs of specific services if the efficiency of service delivery is to be monitored. This is in turn linked to the need for more effective auditing at the local level.

- Personnel management must be improved. Salaries are the largest item of local government expenditure, yet they are frequently wasted through overstaffing, particularly in unskilled positions. Too little remains to offer competitive salaries for key professional staff.

These improvements also imply changes in the central government. Even in countries with autonomous local governments, central governments must retain enough control over aggregate public sector revenue and expenditure to carry out macroeconomic policy. Central governments have legitimate interests in the sectoral allocation of local expenditure, particularly those that impose costs or benefits on surrounding jurisdictions. This degree of central control can be achieved without undermining local accountability, provided the objectives of regulation are clear, and controls are exercised systematically.

Any reallocation of responsibility for urban finance and service provision should be evaluated, therefore, with the following potential conflicts in mind:

- Local objectives may not necessarily be consistent with national objectives.
- There may be insufficient local capacity to perform the financial and technical responsibilities to be assigned to local institutions.
- Local control over resources requires procedures to minimize corruption and abuse of power—i.e., to ensure accountability for resource use.

These concerns do not argue against a reallocation of municipal authority, but they do recognize the complexity and the political difficulties of the process. Autonomy must be balanced by appropriate financial and organizational control, which should operate as incentives for responsible behavior at the local level. This implies the need for a positive approach to this process by national authorities. Such an approach should include, among others, the following:

- Central governments should issue clear standards and guidelines to establish expectations of local performance and help local authorities meet their responsibilities;
- Central governments should involve municipal authorities in formulating the policies and standards that will affect them.
- Central governments should retain some degree of oversight to

Manila, the Philippines.
A community meets to
discuss slum upgrading.

ensure accountability over some areas of local decision making, such as use of investment funds.

- Central governments should actively seek to reinforce local capacities through secondment of central staff to the local level and through training.

These elements do not by themselves ensure effective decentralization. But they would send a positive signal to local authorities that central authorities wish the process to succeed.

A further implicit objective in bringing public responsibility closer to the city is to increase the involvement of community groups in municipal decision making and service provision. The active role and political power of community groups in cities in developing countries, as in the case of Lima described by de Soto,[15] make it imperative for local governance and provision of urban infrastructure and services to be participatory. Past urban policies have frequently forced communities to survive outside the legal framework of the city. In the 1990s, it is no longer politically acceptable to these increasingly powerful groups.

In sum, the process of strengthening the financial and technical capacity of municipal institutions involves many dimensions at both the central and local government levels. Most governments have experimented with aspects of this process and stopped, frequently for political reasons. Others, particularly in Latin America, have persisted in the decentralization process. Involvement of external assistance is certainly not required on what is a politicized issue. Nevertheless, many governments have sought assistance on parts of this process. If they consider it useful, they should continue to be able to call on external expertise where appropriate.

---

15. de Soto (1989).

Box 11. Mortgage Indexation

The fixed-payment mortgage has been a dominant mortgage instrument in many countries over the post-World War II period. However, this instrument does not perform well during periods of high and volatile inflation. Two problems have been identified. The first involves the behavior of lenders. They are reluctant to commit funds for a long period of time at a fixed interest rate when inflation and interest rates are volatile. Numerous alternatives to the standard fixed-payment loan instrument have been developed and adopted during the past fifteen years to combat this problem. In particular, the use of variable rate or adjustable rate instruments has expanded to offer more protection to the lender.

The second problem concerns the demand side—the behavior of borrowers—and the level, not the volatility, of inflation. When inflation is high, interest rates are high and nominal incomes grow annually. The use of a fixed-payment mortgage during such periods results in a mismatch between the stream of income of the family and mortgage payments. The mortgage payments are fixed in nominal terms whereas the family's income increases in nominal terms over the life of the loan. This mismatch increases the share of household income required to pay off a loan under a 10 percent rate of inflation. The amount of income needed in the first year to pay off the same loan amount almost doubles relative to the amount needed to pay off an indexed loan. This "tilting" of the real value of payments toward the early years of a loan in effect makes housing unaffordable even at a 10 percent rate of inflation.

Indexation of mortgage repayments is not a substitute for control of inflation. When inflation accelerates to very high levels no financial instrument is effective, and indexed mortgage contracts are no exception. The risks are simply too great. However, carefully structured indexed mortgages can play an important role in making housing more affordable and contribute to the competitiveness and efficiency of the financial system.

Improve Financial Services for Urban Development

The city is an important user of resources, particularly of a long-term nature, but it is an underused source for the mobilization of financial resources. All too often government transfers have replaced the borrowing of households and municipalities. Not only has this pattern contributed to expansion of the public sector, but it has also ignored an opportunity to develop the private sector. National resource mobilization and expenditure strategies should therefore incorporate the potential contributions of urban households, communities, and urban local governments.

This involves assessing the linkages between the financial sector and the financing needs of urban populations and urban institutions. Financial sector policies to mobilize domestic savings, for example, should exploit the opportunities to increase private household savings in cities, through the design of appropriate savings instruments and interest rate policies. In Colombia, the introduction of indexed mortgages stimulated competition for financial resources. It reduced the burden of inflationary taxes on monetary balances and thereby contributed substantially to the growth of the financial system as well as the economy.

The major need for financial services has been in the housing sector. Improving housing finance requires strengthening or substantially restructuring housing finance policies and institutions. Housing finance policies have usually included significant subsidies and therefore are not neutral in their allocation of resources within the financial sector. Moreover, they can have both direct and indirect negative consequences for household savings. Therefore, one objective in strengthening financial services should be to target subsidies more efficiently and transparently to the very poor, in place of broad unsustainable financial subsidies resulting from earlier policies. This is an important part of overall housing sector reform because it redefines the role of government in enabling and supporting private investment. While developing self-sustaining systems for those groups who can afford formal housing finance, subsidies can still be provided to those who need assistance. More careful policy design, however, can allow many more households to be served without adding major new distortions to the housing market or the financial sector. Financial policies, therefore, should complement user charges and other cost-recovery mechanisms in mobilizing private savings, thereby contributing to reducing the overall role of government in the sector.

The pricing of credit to reflect the opportunity cost of capital elsewhere in the economy should also improve efficiency of public sector resource allocation. Municipal borrowing for infrastructure financed by central government should be as close to a market rate as possible. Many countries are now attempting to reform their municipal credit systems, raising interest rate levels to reflect market rates. Countries such as India and some states in Brazil have promoted near-market interest rates as a key part of their reform of local infrastructure finance. The establishment of municipal development funds as a mechanism to allocate public resources for local investment purposes has potential to help rationalize this process. These experiments need to be evaluated to ensure that they are sustainable, without inefficient administrative costs and implicit credit subsidies.

Box 12. Bridging Informal Norms and Formal Financial Sector Requirements in India

A contentious issue in many developing countries is the development of fair and efficient ways to resolve loan-repayment disputes between lower income borrowers and large, usually government-sponsored, financial institutions. The importance of this issue increases in countries where lenders have traditionally been large landowners who lent at high real interest rates to borrowers who were often landless peasants living at near subsistence levels. In such environments, formal sector legal protections often provide so much protection that no formal sector lending takes place.

The Indian approach to loan-dispute resolution is a good example of formal sector policy that ultimately did not provide protection for the borrowers it was designed to help. A Government of India study showed that it takes ten years or more to resolve mortgage contract disputes. As a result, rather than protecting borrowers, the legal system actually discouraged formal mortgage lending.

The Housing Development Finance Company of India (HDFC) has now operated for more than ten years in this kind of environment, making more than 400,000 mortgage loans at market interest rates. Remarkably, although most of the loans have been made to lower- and moderate-income households, and have an average size of less than US$4,000, they have produced a delinquency rate of less than 1/2 of 1 percent. This is a rate that compares favorably with the experience of lenders in more developed economies: the U.S. Federal Housing Authority (FHA) experiences a 7 percent default rate on its unsubsidized insured loans.

HDFC has accomplished this record by circumventing, but not avoiding, the formal mechanisms for dealing with loan disputes. It has focused on moral suasion outside of the legal system—in particular, on borrowers' concerns with their reputations. Third-party guarantees are sought on almost all loans. The third party is always someone the borrower respects—e.g., an older colleague or a relative. Like the borrower, the guarantor also has to submit a financial statement to demonstrate an ability to repay the loan in the event that the borrower cannot. If loans are not repaid promptly and the borrower's explanation for tardiness is unsatisfactory, the threat of calling on the guarantor for repayment is raised, and ultimately followed through in the face of further recalcitrance on the borrower's part. If this induces no response, legal action is initiated.

Ultimately, HFDC has rarely relied on the formal legal code to provide the basis for effective contract enforcement. Its success is a result of bridging informal cultural norms to fulfill contracts with the formal financial sector needs. Its excellent record of loan recovery provides the credibility essential to convince formal sector financial investors that deposits in the corporation are safe. By establishing a new "custom" of appropriate behavior, it has made such informal activities attractive investments.

Agenda Item II: Alleviating Urban Poverty

Chapter II noted the two-part strategy recommended by the *World Development Report 1990*. It requires an attack on both the economic and social aspects of poverty. This strategy includes increasing the labor productivity of the poor through incentives, institutions, infrastructure, and technology, as well as increased social sector expenditure for human resource development. Urban policies and programs to date have combined these strategies and made some progress particularly in providing shelter and services to the urban poor in cities such as Jakarta, Calcutta, and Bombay. The adoption of more effective mechanisms to deliver shelter, infrastructure, and social services has helped to reduce costs and improve the access of the poor. However, most slum upgrading and sites-and-services projects have had relatively little effect on the magnitude of the problem. In addition, an effective strategy to help the poor must distinguish those groups that have suffered from the transitional impacts of adjustment programs from those affected by the longer term problems of access to services and low productivity.

The Economic Aspects of Poverty: Increasing Labor Productivity

An important first step toward increasing labor productivity is to address public policies affecting the demand for labor. Government policies influencing labor-intensive productive activities have clear impacts on the poor. At the macroeconomic level, experience has shown, for example, that increased government protection for domestic industries also increases the capital intensity of production, with the consequence of fewer employment opportunities being generated for the poor. A more neutral trade regime tends to increase the demand for labor in the industrial sector.

At the city level, governments should pay particular attention to regulations that tend to prevent the growth of productivity of urban entrepreneurs and should provide greater incentives and improved services to meet their needs. (See box 14.) This is particularly true of the informal sector whose contribution to the urban economy has become increasingly appreciated in most cities in developing countries. The dynamism and effectiveness of the informal sector, in overcoming hostile legal systems and local institutions is remarkable. It demonstrates the inhibiting influence of the state in many situations, or at least the inefficiencies caused by government intervention.

The structural constraints of laws and regulations that limit the access of small-scale entrepreneurs to infrastructure, credit, and markets need to be directly addressed. As de Soto has described in the case of Lima,

Box 13. Reaching Poor Women in Urban Projects

Two World Bank-assisted urban projects in Ethiopia include small innovative components to assist poor women in urban areas with a particular
emphasis on cost recovery. These projects aim at utilizing the entrepre-
neurial capacities of women for generating income in poor urban areas.
One of them is the Second Addis Ababa Urban Development Project,
which includes a component to assist poor women living in the Kebele
(slum) areas to undertake revenue-generating projects. Up to 15 percent
(US$165,000) of the Kebele Development Fund is earmarked for income
generation for poor women. Subloans will be provided to eligible women
on the basis of a detailed feasibility study to be carried out by the Addis
Ababa Administrative Region (AAAR). Meanwhile, AAAR will engage in
discussions with the women's associations and inititate prospective proposals for loans. Loan funds are expected to be used in activities such as
preparing foodstuffs for restaurants, pottery work, sewing training, and
purchase of equipment. These loans are expected to be repaid anytime
within six years.

The Market Towns Development Project in Ethiopia also has an experimental income enhancement/entrepreneurship development program
for women. A total credit of US$1.4 million, is planned for disbursement
through the Agricultural and Industrial Development Bank (AIDB), and
the technical assistance will occur through the Handicrafts and Small
Industry Development Agency (HASIDA) to micro-scale, cottage industry
and service enterprises, which will be organized into cooperatives. Primary beneficiaries of this support will be women-owned cottage industries
and women school leavers. HASIDA and AIDB will further initiate a
savings program for the micro-scale cooperative members and facilitate
cost recovery.

regulatory constraints prevent small entrepreneurs from legalizing and
expanding their firms. Similarly, local-level initiatives to extend credit
through nonformal banking institutions can assist even the poorest
individuals and households in establishing economic enterprises. (See
box 13.) If these constraints can be accurately identified and reduced, the
likelihood will increase that the poor can take advantage of opportunities
within the urban economy. For poor women, particularly those who
head households, the biggest constraint is the time required for domestic
responsibilities. A recent income-generating project in Colombia increased women's labor productivity by including a community-run
child-care component in the project.

The Social Aspects of Poverty: Investing in the Human Capital and Basic Needs of the Poor

Increasing social sector expenditure for human resource development
requires medium- and longer-term national investment in education,

Bangkok, Thailand. An improved low-income settlement along the klongs.

health, nutrition, and family planning to improve the labor productivity and incomes of urban households. While data on average access to schools, clinics, and other services usually show that urban areas are privileged relative to rural areas, significant intraurban disparities exist in these services in most cities. Data in Bangkok, Mexico City, and Lusaka demonstrate the need to increase the availability of these services in the settlements inhabited by the poor. The position of women and children is most critical, given the complex mutually reinforcing effects of education and health care on family size, labor force participation, and income levels. Government strategies in these sectors need to devote special attention to the lack of access experienced by particular groups within the urban population.

An important complement to increased human capital investment is the need for improved access by the poor to basic infrastructure and housing. These determine the environment in which improved health and productivity can occur. While the sites-and-services programs of the 1970s and 1980s reduced the costs of shelter and infrastructure, they did not usually reach the poorest households. In cases where very poor families obtained plots, they frequently sold them to middle-income people to gain a windfall. It is important to note that, despite claims to the contrary, sites-and-services projects proved to be highly subsidized, with prices to project participants far below market prices. Cost recovery was not achieved. In contrast, the squatter-upgrading or slum-improvement programs were more successful in providing benefits to the poor while ensuring security of tenure. Programs in many cities such as Calcutta, Bamako, and Manila, successfully created better served environments in which the poor could gradually improve their quality of life.

Cost recovery also worked relatively better than in the sites-and-services areas. It is recommended that governments continue to upgrade the unserviced settlements inhabited by the poor.

Successful upgrading of existing neighborhoods should also be complemented by changing building codes and regulations that exclude poor households from access to credit for construction loans. Despite many efforts to rewrite these codes and regulations, they remain in force in most countries. The problem of the homeless in many situations is attributable to codes that require larger investments in dwellings than would be affordable by low-income people.

Another important component is support of the efforts of community and nongovernmental organizations to provide services in their neighborhoods. All cities in developing countries have active community groups that have sought to meet household and community needs in the face of ineffective government policy and scarce public resources. These activities include (i) encouraging the formation of community leadership, both male and female, to represent and inform communities and to intermediate between communities and government; (ii) performing technical roles in shelter provision such as the purchase of building materials or finance of shelter; (iii) training communities for self-reliance; and (iv) maintaining infrastructure and social services.

Central and local governments, therefore, should provide technical and financial support to community initiatives to the extent possible. These organizations and their activities obviously have political significance at the local level, but enabling them to meet community needs and provide services can generate positive political relationships.

Targeting "Safety Net" Assistance to the Poor

Targeting "safety net" assistance to those most vulnerable to shocks among the urban population—largely children and women, and particularly those who head households—is a high priority. In the past, assistance to the poor within cities has usually been considered in terms of subsidized shelter and water supply. This approach needs to be broadened. Choices must be made on an urgent basis at the national and city levels as to whether and how to target subsidies for food, energy, shelter, and water for the poorest urban households. Three principles should be followed in these choices: First, subsidies should be transparent. Secondly, they should avoid creating price distortions in other markets, as with interest rates. Finally, they should occur before construction, as in the case of housing subsidies in Chile, and not through mortgage payments over time.

These principles have been followed in the creative nutrition programs

---

Box 14. Microenterprises in Kumasi, Ghana

There is an area called Suame Magazine, only two miles from the center of Kumasi, where about 2,000 small entrepreneurs are crowded at one location and engaged in a wide range of activities such as auto repairs, machine tool cutting, drilling, welding, paint and spray work, and electrical work. These microenterprises, typically with a master and three or four apprentices, are industrious, innovative, and hard-working. The enterprises occupy a small plot (40 by 80 to 60 by 120 feet) and undertake these activities under extremely adverse conditions, especially without basic infrastructure services. As this area gets easily flooded, the drainage problems are serious. The roads are bumpy and unpaved and without easy access to main roads. Electrical supply exists, but distribution and transmission facilities are lacking. Water connections need to be extended. The disposal of waste materials is also a major problem.

These microenterprises have the potential to grow and generate additional employment, but their growth is seriously limited by: (i) inadequate infrastructure services, (ii) lack of general education and managerial skills, (iii) lack of business services and market information, (iv) lack of access to credit to purchase tools and equipment, (v) uncertainties about the future business climate, and (vi) unavailability of sites for expansion. Greater incentives, better infrastructure, and business services are badly needed. In contrast, large-scale establishments can afford to internalize externalities; by doing so, however, they contribute little to developing industrial structure with vertical linkages. Moreover, their plant expansion, often with automation of facilities, tends to contribute little to employment generation (World Bank, 1989b).

---

in Brazil and Colombia. The programs demonstrate that the poorest households in Latin America can be spared from malnutrition. In the Colombian Community Child Nutrition and Development Project, nutritional supplements covering 80 percent of the daily nutritional requirement were targeted to more than one million children from the lowest income quintile. Other targeted assistance in Mozambique, Tanzania, Mexico, Guatemala, and Haiti demonstrated that when institutional bottlenecks to service delivery can be overcome, urgent short-term benefits can be provided to the most needy groups. Declining urban per capita incomes have resulted in a problem of urban malnutrition. Even in countries such as Pakistan, which experienced sustained real economic growth rates of over 6 percent during the 1980s, child malnutrition increased by 20 percent. Whether and how food subsidies might be targeted to the poor should depend on individual country and city circumstances and should be understood as part of overall urban and subsidy policy.

Regardless of the strategy adopted, it is clear that, in the short term, the bright lights of the city have dimmed and are, for many urban households, extinguished. The challenge is to manage the transitional costs of economic change and to cushion the most vulnerable groups. In the long term, however, the costs of forgoing necessary investments in the short-term in food, health, and education for the poor will be large with respect to population growth, environmental degradation, and declining national productivity.

Taking the short- and long-term perspectives together, improving the productivity of the urban economy during adjustment will shorten the period of economic transition and thus alleviate poverty. If productivity can be maintained and increased, urban employment and incomes can be expected to grow. Addressing the worst aspects of this economic transition in terms of increased prices of food, energy, water supply, and health care can play a major role in both meeting short-term needs and ensuring some of the inputs needed to keep the urban population healthy and productive.

Agenda Item III: Developing Effective Responses to the Growing Urban Environmental Crisis

Increase Awareness of the Urban Environmental Crisis

In recent years a large amount of international attention has been directed to worldwide environmental issues such as global warming, depletion of the ozone layer, acid rain, and deforestation. Urban areas are major contributors to these problems because of the intensity of energy and other resource use and the concentration of wastes and emissions. Whereas the global problems are serious, the full scope of their consequences has yet to be revealed. In contrast, the harsh impacts of urban environmental problems on the health and productivity of individuals, households, and communities are already dramatically evident. Increasing international awareness of these local environmental issues will be fundamental to mobilizing the resources needed to address the problems.

The growing urban environmental crisis requires a range of difficult measures from the responsible national, regional, and local authorities. Effective political commitment to local environmental improvement will therefore be essential.

Develop an Information Base and Understanding of the Dynamics of Urban Environmental Deterioration

A striking feature of the urban environmental crisis is the relative lack of accurate information. Environmental degradation is complex. It involves economic and social pressures beyond the natural environment's ability to withstand those effects. Institutions need information on economic and social activity that leads to environmental degradation. Information is also needed on the absorptive capacity of the natural environment and the consequent environmental conditions. There is also a need for information about the types and costs of possible interventions and their effectiveness. For example, whereas data are available on air pollution in Sao Paulo, there are almost no data on air pollution in any African city. Where data are collected, there is little capacity to ensure their quality and comparability with other data. This makes it difficult to identify long-term programs of priority actions and regulatory policies. It also limits the possibility of any assessment of change because no baseline data exist. It is thus critical for central and local governments to invest in establishing agencies and systems for collection of environmental data and monitoring of changes in air, water, and soil conditions.

This investment is also a first step toward developing an understanding of the dynamics of environmental deterioration in specific cities. Without such an analytic understanding of the causes of deterioration, designing effective programs and policies will be impossible.

Despite the need for information in the design of long-term programs and policies and assessment of their impacts, it is important to stress that this requirement should not preclude immediate action in the short term where problems are evident and where there is little risk that environmental protection measures will create additional problems. Indeed, examples abound of natural resources that are deteriorating as a result of behaviors induced by uneconomic prices. Changing such prices could have important short-term impacts on environmentally unsound practices.

Develop City-Specific Strategies for Environmental Management

It is essential that national and local governments formulate city-specific strategies for environmental management. For example, environmental studies of Izmir, Turkey, illustrate that local authorities will have to make difficult trade-offs in their decisions about the use of scarce water supplies and their impact on Izmir's tourism industry. Recent initiatives for air-quality improvements in Mexico City involving reducing the number of vehicular trips, improving the quality of fuels, installing catalytic converters on all cars, and establishing systems for monitoring air quality are good examples of local efforts to develop such strategies. The Magic Eyes campaign in Bangkok (whereby children have been organized to collect and prevent litter) is another example of using community resources to improve environmental conditions.

Identify High-Priority Curative Actions

Governments should identify high-priority curative actions required to address existing problems. Curative action should safeguard public health in the short term by addressing problems such as inadequate domestic wastewater treatment and disposal, industrial water and air pollution, air pollution from urban transport sources, and inadequate solid-waste collection and disposal. Curative action will probably require investments for pollution abatement, especially sewage treatment and the treatment of industrial wastes. Partial interventions should be avoided (e.g., water supply without sanitation, storm drainage without solid-waste management). Given the high cost of investment, service standards should be designed in accordance with affordability and willingness to pay in different areas of the city.

Establish Preventive Policies and Incentives

Preventive policies are needed to confront longer term threats to the urban environment. Among the threats are the risk of irreversible damage to resources and ecosystems and endangering the possibility of sustainable economic development. This includes the depletion or contamination of surface water and groundwater resources. It also includes possible irreversible damage to coastal areas, erosion-prone areas, and wetlands through uncontrolled development or improper disposal of toxic and hazardous wastes.

Especially because of the difficulties of enforcing environmental regulations, incentive systems should be considered, where feasible, to encourage good environmental behavior. For example, pricing policies are needed for land, water, energy, minerals, and food that encourage conservation by urban consumers and contribute to resource protection. By pricing resources and services at cost, excessive resource use can be discouraged and costly investments postponed. In the case of energy and some industrial inputs, especially in countries with seriously distorted prices, improved pricing policies can be an incentive for more efficient resource use and reduced air and water pollution. In most cases, much more research is needed to understand how to design more effective incentive systems for protecting the urban environment.

Improved urban planning and enforcement are often necessary to protect environmentally sensitive areas. A protection program for marginal lands may include the use of a balance of economic incentives and urban planning regulations. These would include policies to improve the functioning of land markets (e.g., appropriate land-use and land-development regulations and more effective land-tenure and land-registration systems) and to improve access by the poor to serviced land, thereby reducing the pressure on marginal land. In most cases, much more research is needed to understand how to design more effective incentive systems for protecting the urban environment.

Regulation and Enforcement

Local governments usually have to enforce environmental protection regulations established by the central government. This implies the need to design environmental regulations with close collaboration between central and municipal governments. In many countries, the achievement of effective local/national coordination on standards and enforcement has proved difficult. More analysis is required in many countries to design realistic environmental standards and effective enforcement mechanisms. Standards must be accepted by the public, because success requires public cooperation. Building a broad public awareness of environmental issues is essential, but it takes time. Regulatory systems should enable communities and the private sector, including the informal sector, to supply environmental services. Solid-waste collection and disposal, for example, are managed in many cities in industrial countries by the private sector.

Given the importance of enforcement, it is important to consider ways of improving performance. These may include:

- Developing codes and standards that are easy to understand and assess in order to minimize disagreements about compliance or enforcement. The codes and standards would be supported by resources needed for implementation.
- Upgrading the status and pay of the civil servants responsible for enforcement. This should reduce disputes and attract more competent people to the job.
- Working with industry, communities, and nongovernmental organizations (NGOs) to increase awareness and shared responsibility for environmental resources.
- Using international expertise when local capacity cannot be developed quickly or effectively.

Agenda Item IV: Increase Urban Research

A final item of the urban agenda for the 1990s is the need to increase the understanding of urban issues. In contrast to the extensive investment made in urban research during the 1970s, the decade of the 1980s has seen a decline in the quantity of urban research in both developed and developing countries. Past research had important operational benefits. Studies on squatter settlements in Latin America, for example, led to powerful insights about the importance of land tenure as an incentive for private investment in housing. Studies of household incomes in Asia and Africa led to an appreciation of affordability of shelter and infrastructure. The research-and-development process has been an important part of understanding the city. Yet, in the 1980s, the scarcity of public resources for research, coupled with increasing interest in other subjects such as debt and adjustment, led to an unfortunate decline in research at a time when many urban policy questions were becoming increasingly important. At the same time, the dramatic changes in urban growth and the composition of urban activities over the past decade have put much of the earlier work out of date.

The policy framework presented in Chapter II is based on three analytical elements: (i) the interrelationships between the urban economy and macroeconomic performance through the fiscal, financial, and real sector linkages; (ii) a set of political, institutional, regulatory, and financial constraints that inhibit exploiting the productive potential of urban households and enterprises to the fullest extent; and (iii) the probable policy impacts on urban productivity, relative welfare of the poor, and the environmental conditions. Such a framework implies a need to conduct extensive research in key areas. At the same time it offers a rich menu for future research. The following key areas have been identified:

- *The Urban Economy and Macroeconomic Aggregates.* There is a need to articulate clearly the interrelationships between the performance of the urban economy and macro-aggregates, since the former can affect significantly not only economic growth but also macroeconomic stability, including inflation, unemployment, and national savings. More specific research could include (i) urban infrastructure investment and its contribution to growth, (ii) the role of housing finance in macroeconomic stability in the short run, and its potential contribution to savings and resource mobilization in the long run; and (iii) local government finance and its contribution to the fiscal performance of the national government.
- *Internal Efficiencies of Cities and Urban Productivity.* There is an increasing need to understand clearly the functioning of megacities, since the interactions among different actors (e.g., households, firms, and public agencies) are becoming more complex and probable effects of policy interventions are becoming more difficult to predict. As has been noted, questions increasingly arise about the limits to the agglomeration benefits associated with megacities. Research could be directed to (i) the functioning of the urban markets, including land, housing, and labor, focusing particularly on the regulatory and institutional constraints; (ii) effects of public

infrastructure investments (such as urban transport, water supply, electric power and telecommunications) on urban growth patterns, since inconsistencies between new investments and location dynamics will induce inefficiencies and welfare loss; and (iii) the effects of urban investments on residential and employment location nexuses, since they will determine the commuting patterns and overall spatial development pattern.

- *The Urban Poor and the Informal Sector.* The productivity of low-income families in urban areas is constrained by limited urban services and amenities that characterize the informal sector in which they operate. The need exists to understand the nature of the constraints that can be mitigated to improve the productive potential of the poor. Research could assess alternative approaches to the delivery of basic services. A more challenging task would be to understand the mechanisms by which community- based productive activities are carried out. New insights are needed for expediting these innovative processes observed in the informal sector of urban areas.

- *Financing of Urban Investments.* Maintenance and delivery of urban services are seriously constrained by the lack of financial resources of the governments at both the national and local level. New areas of research should include (i) local governments' participation in financial markets, (ii) deregulation and private sector participation in the supply of infrastructure services, and (iii) the complementarity between public and private investments.

- *The Role of Government in the Urban Development Process.* The efficient functioning of urban markets and the productivity of individual households and firms are affected by the political structure, various institutional settings, and the locus of decision making within the structure. There is a need to better understand the nature of these tensions within the existing structure in such a way that broad-based institutional reforms can be achieved. An immediate research task in this area is to develop such a framework for institutional reform in Eastern Europe. Sequencing of housing-finance reform, for example, will be predicated on the speed of overall macroeconomic reform, but also on the emerging institutional framework.

- *Urban Environment.* Cities offer positive externalities generated by high-density economic activities. At the same time, negative externalities such as traffic congestion and pollution seriously affect the health and productivity of individual urban dwellers. Very little is known of the probable impacts of government intervention on the balance between these two outcomes. Research could address improved zoning and pollution and congestion taxes. Conservation of natural resources and more efficient resource use also deserve more research.

This list needs to be refined on the basis of an assessment of the current state of urban research. The last partial assessment of urban research capacity in the developing countries was supported by the Ford Foundation in the early 1970s. The Ford Foundation has recently agreed to finance regional assessments in Africa and Latin America. These will be undertaken by senior local researchers in the coming year. On the basis of these assessments, a long-term urban research strategy should be formulated by these local specialists together with representatives of international agencies and specialists from developed countries. The strategy should distinguish between short- and long-term research topics. It should also identify priority subjects for different regions and countries.

Part of the assessment of urban research should include an evaluation of the resources available. On the basis of extensive discussions in developing countries over the past two years, there appears to be an urgent need to mobilize a substantially higher level of resources for urban research. This view was corroborated in an April 1990 workshop of major U.S. foundations to discuss urban issues in developing countries and the possibility of launching an International Consortium for Urban Research. The future of this initiative would depend on the above assessments.

There is also a need to foster the development of a broad-based learning strategy for urban issues. This includes studying how communities can learn from one another within cities and how innovations from one city can be evaluated and, if appropriate, diffused to other cities. Much of this process will not come through formal hypothesis testing but through "action-research" involving urban residents, NGOs, and public institutions themselves. However, such a process will not occur without support from international, national, or local institutions.

4

Strategy for the World Bank

The broadened urban agenda for the developing countries in the 1990s represents a challenge to the World Bank to further the evolution in Bank urban lending from demonstration projects toward establishing national and city-level policies that increase the contribution of the urban economy and urban institutions to national development objectives. The areas for policy reform are largely, but not exclusively, citywide. National sectoral policies such as those affecting housing finance or water-supply investment will clearly influence the agenda for city-level reform. Nevertheless, in most cases, the impact and implementation of that agenda will occur at the city level. Strategies to alleviate urban poverty may have neighborhood components, but they must be based on citywide assessments of the most vulnerable groups. The urban environment can be addressed only on a citywide basis.

Operational Work

As noted in Chapter 1, Bank operations in the urban sector since 1972 have played an important role in the response of the international community to rapid urban growth. This has been reflected in many new ideas and in more than a hundred lending operations approved by the Bank's Board through FY90. There is little doubt that much has been accomplished in individual cities through the adoption of new approaches and in targeted investments to improve the delivery of urban shelter and infrastructure. There has been, on the basis of experience, an evolution of objectives for urban assistance during the last two decades.

The current project pipeline indicates that in response to increased requests from countries, Bank urban lending is projected to grow significantly in FY91-93. This lending will develop further in the direction of:

- *Policy reforms*, to improve urban productivity, such as reforms of the

---

Box 15. The Evolution of Urban Projects in Brazil

The Bank's involvement in urban areas in Brazil has been marked by an evolution of focus from a project emphasis to a sector, and, later, a multisector perspective. It has moved from a concern with specific neighborhoods to a concern with single-city sites and multicities to finally the state. The degree of complexity has increased with the number of states, cities, agencies, and sectors involved. The first two projects in urban areas in Brazil, the First Urban Transport Project (1978) and the Sites-and-Services and Low-Cost Housing Project (1979), concentrated on sector-specific types of investment. In 1979, the Medium-Sized Cities Project designed a complicated, yet fairly successful program as Brazil's third urban project. Although the project was multi-agency, city, state, and sectoral, its financial mechanisms allowed local governments greater latitude to design their own programs on the basis of their demonstrated financial and staffing capacities. The next projects, the Recife Metropolitan Regional Development Project (1982), the Santa Catarina Small Towns Improvement Project (1985), and the Salvador Metropolitan Development Project (1986), concentrated their efforts at a regional level. These projects were slightly less complicated in terms of the number of agencies, but more so in political terms. The regional experience in Parana with the Market Towns Improvement Project (1983) and Municipal Development Project (1989) has continued the concentration on institution building and an approach that allows local governments discretion in structuring their programs. All these programs have had varying degrees of success, more so with the physical outputs than with the institutional or policy-related aspects. The record of implementation broadly demonstrated that neither complexity nor simplicity guaranteed success or failure of projects. The macroeconomic and political environments seemed to be of far greater importance than was the degree of technical and administrative complexity of the project. The experience in Brazil demostrates that projects can succeed in a narrow physical sense, but policy directions are less successful when the broader issues of urban development are not tackled.

---

regulatory framework governing land and housing markets, of central-local financial relations, and of financial policies affecting investment in housing and infrastructure;

- *Institutional development,* to strengthen (a) the financial and technical capacities of municipalities, including reinforcement of capacity to operate and maintain citywide infrastructure and services; (b) national institutions involved in the financing of housing and infrastructure; (c) national, regional, and municipal institutions involved in the management of the urban environment, including formulation, monitoring, and enforcement of environmental policies and standards;

- *Investments* in citywide infrastructure networks, including rehabilitation where needed, rather than the neighborhood-specific infrastructure of the past; housing and land development through financial intermediaries who mobilize private savings and private sector involvement, including sites-and-services if appropriate within an overall assessment of the housing market; curative environmental improvements, such as drainage or programs to reduce air pollution; upgrading of existing slum areas; provision of social services, such as health, nutrition, and education to meet basic needs; urban transport facilities, including public or private buses; citywide networks of services such as markets.

Within these categories, lending instruments will include project investment lending or sector investment lending. Lending will support policy reforms, institutional development efforts, and some investments at the city level, while continuing investments in infrastructure subsectors. This assistance will be based on an analysis of the most critical constraints to urban productivity, the alleviation of urban poverty, and the management of the urban environment. Operations will address systemic issues within regional cities as well as the capital city or groups of cities. Where national sector issues are involved, sector lending will be appropriate. The policy content of lending will also be increased as indicated in the following examples:

- *Municipal Development Loans.* While these loans will include policy, institutional, and investment components, in contrast to past municipal development operations, they will also require an effort to improve central-local financial relations. Investment at the municipal level will be conditional on improved central-local relations.
- *Housing Finance Loans.* In contrast to earlier housing finance operations, the conditions for these operations will include assessment of the land and housing markets and regulatory audits in cities in which investment would occur. Understanding these two essential elements of the context for housing finance is necessary for locating housing and residential infrastructure investments. These prior steps will also ensure that the private sector and informal sector roles in shelter and infrastructure provision were understood and explicitly encouraged within the framework of investment operations.

In both examples, the policy and institutional content will define the context for investment. While this increased policy and institutional content might be considered too ambitious, it is evident from Bank experience that strengthening the linkages between the national and municipal levels is essential for success.

As part of country economic and sector work and project preparation, reasonable urban policy and institutional objectives will be identified within individual countries and cities. These objectives will be agreed upon with borrowers and then serve as benchmarks against which future lending will be considered. In effect, it is proposed that country-specific performance criteria be adopted for the urban sector, such as municipal revenue performance, improvement in maintenance of municipal services, an level of housing subsidies. This process will be based on increased urban sector work, with particular attention to the impacts of urban policy on urban economic activities and in turn on macroeconomic performance.

Aid Coordination

The Bank's sectoral policy contribution will continue to be provided in the context of the Development Assistance Committee of the O.E.C.D. and in Bank representation at the United Nations' Habitat Commission (UNCHS). Country-level aid coordination will also become increasingly important. The follow-up to the Bank report *Sub-Saharan Africa: From Crisis to Sustainable Growth* will result in sectoral discussions among donors. This type of regional initiative should be complemented at the country level through consortia, round tables, and other discussions of aid coordination.

In view of the growing appreciation of urban issues and increased urban activity by the international community, the Development Assis-

---

Box 16. Urban Sector Lending in Indonesia

The need for adjustment in the Indonesian economy resulted in a recognition that public financing had to be restructured. An important aspect of this restructuring was to promote greater local responsibility for planning, financing and maintaining local infrastructure. This recognition resulted in actions on the part of the government that created opportunities for revising central-local financial relationships and devolution of responsibilities from the center to the regional and local levels. The Bank and other donors provided assistance to the government in this context that may have furthered these objectives. In 1987, the Bank granted the Government of Indonesia an urban sector loan with a total value of US$270 million. Continuing to assist the Government's reforms will involve developing the understanding and capacity within the Bank and other donors to identify and encourage activities in key opportunity areas. Within this sector policy framework, urban development projects are under preparation for Kalimantan and East Java.

tance Committee held its first urban meeting in 1986. A second meeting will be held in 1992. Recent donor meetings in Ottawa (1988) and Lille, France (1989), have emphasized the need for joint approaches to policy formulation and assistance.

To develop a common approach to urban problems, the World Bank initiated an Urban Management Program jointly with UNCHS and UNDP in 1986. This program is a research and technical-assistance program covering land development, municipal finance, infrastructure management, and environment. Its second phase has been approved by UNDP, with core funding of US$2.1 million for two years and with a commitment for another six years beyond CY91. The program has received additional support from the United Kingdom, Germany, Switzerland, Finland, and France to date, with parallel activities financed by the United States and Canada.

Research

In Chapter III the need to increase urban research was presented as the fourth agenda. The priority research areas are identified within the policy framework developed in this paper. However, the range of questions extend beyond the capacity of the Bank to undertake urban research in the medium term. Given the weakness of urban research capacity in the developing countries, the assessment of urban research during 1991–92 will help to determine whether there is a need for increased international financial support.

Within the Bank, the urban research program includes projects under the following headings:

- *The Urban Economy and Macroeconomic Aggregates*: research examining the impact of infrastructure constraints on the productivity and growth of industries in Indonesia and Thailand, the sequencing of housing sector reform in Eastern Europe, the composition of urban public investment and its impact on private investment, and the mobilization of local financial resources.
- *Internal Efficiencies of Cities and Urban Productivity*: research examining the impact of regulation on land markets and alternative approaches to improving land market efficiency, and the development of performance indicators for the housing sector.
- *Urban Poverty and the Informal Sector*: research examining the impact of structural adjustment policies on poor urban households, with particular attention to impacts within the households, such as on women and children.
- *The Urban Environment*: research on the health impacts of urbanization and the strategic options for urban environmental policy.

Box 17. The Urban Management Program

The World Bank is undertaking a program of research and technical assistance, the Urban Management Program (UMP) in collaboration with the United Nations Center for Human Settlements (UNCHS) with financing from UNDP and several bilateral donors. The Program includes analysis of issues in urban land management, in the operation and maintenance of urban infrastructure, in municipal finance and management, and urban environment. The program has been motivated by a conscious effort to shift awareness from the provision of housing and residential infrastructure to broader policies related to urban management.

During the first phase of the Program, case studies were undertaken in connection with UNCHS and World Bank projects. This work has contributed to a changing emphasis in many Bank-assisted urban projects. There are now, for example, thirty-nine projects that seek to improve the administration of urban property taxes, many of which have benefited directly from the UMP.

The UMP is developing a methodology for land market evaluation and for evaluating how possible improvements in land development and construction standards, land tenure, land registration, and land information systems can improve the functioning of land markets. This work has contributed to an improved understanding of appropriate policies for different economic, legal, and cultural settings. A separate component is undertaking case studies to assess appropriate systems and methodologies for the operation and maintenance of infrastructure.

Work on the urban environment will identify the main types of environmental problems in cities such as inadequate household-waste collection, treatment and disposal, pollution from industrial wastes, and water-resource degradation. It will also analyze the impacts of environmental problems and their causes (e.g., regulatory failure, inappropriate pricing policies, insufficient investment in treatment) and suggest appropriate strategies for dealing with them.

The next phase will focus on "capacity building" for research and training at the regional, national, and local levels. This will include holding "urban management consultations" with governments to identify high priority policy and institutional issues to be addressed by urban assistance.

This list represents a significant increase in Bank urban research, yet it only touches on some of the priority issues identified earlier. Clearly a major effort will be needed to expand urban research outside of the Bank.

Another area deserving renewed emphasis is evaluation of urban assistance programs. The Bank conducted in-depth evaluations of a sample of projects in the 1970s, such as the joint evaluation with IDRC of Bank-assisted projects in Senegal, El Salvador, Zambia, and the Philippines, and subsequently undertook other individual project evaluations. This work will be significantly expanded in the future.

Bibliography

Agarwala, Ramgopal. *Price Distortions and Growth in Developing Countries*. World Bank Staff Working Paper No. 575, 1983.

Aschauer, David. *Is Public Expenditure Productive?* Federal Reserve Bank of Chicago Staff Memorandum. 1989.

Bapat, Meera, Nigel Crook, and G.R. Malaker. *The Impact of Environment and Economic Class on Health in Urban India: Case Studies of Pune and Durgapur*. University of London, 1989.

Briscoe, John. *Adult Health in Brazil: Adjusting to New Challenges*. Report No. 7807-BR, 1989.

Buckley, Robert, and Stephen K. Mayo. *Housing and the Macroeconomy*. Review of Regional and Development Studies. 1(2), 1989.

Caplovitz, David C. *The Poor Pay More*. New York: The Free Press, 1967.

Carroll, Alan. *Pirate Subdivisions and the Market for Residential Lots in Bogota*. World Bank Staff Working Paper No. 435, 1980.

Cohen, Michael A. *Learning by Doing: World Bank Lending for Urban Development, 1972-82*. World Bank, 1983.

de Soto, Hernando. *The Other Path*. New York: Harper and Row, 1989.

Dowall, David E. Land *and Housing Assessment: An Important Tool for Increasing Housing Delivery in Third World Cities*, Habitat International, V 12, No.4, 1988

Friedman, Benjamin. "Postwar Changes in American Financial Markets," in Martin Feldstein, ed., *The American Economy in Transition*. University of Chicago Press, 1980.

Global Environmental Monitoring System. *Global Pollution and Health: Results of Health-Related Environmental Monitoring*. London: United Nations Environmental Program and the World Health Organization, 1987.

Gordon, Ian. *Housing and Labor Market Constraints Across the North South Divide*. Paper prepared for the IIESR Conference on Housing and the National Economy, 1988.

Harpham, Trudy, Tim Lusty, and Patrick Vaughan. *In the Shadow of the City: Community Health and the Urban Poor*. Oxford University Press, 1988.

Hardoy, Jorge and David Satterthwaite. *Squatter Citizen: Life in the Urban Third World*. London: Earthscan Publications, 1989.

Hughes, G.A. and B. McCormick. *Housing and Labor Market Performance*. Paper prepared for the IIESR Conference on Housing and the National Economy, 1988.

International Labor Office. *Yearbook of Labor Statistics, 1988*. Geneva, 1988.

Kahnert, Friedrich. *Improving Urban Employment and Labor Productivity*. World Bank Discussion Paper No. 10, May 1987.

Landell-Mills, Pierre, Ramgopal Agarwala, and Stanley Please. *Sub-Saharan Africa: From Crisis to Sustainable Growth*. World Bank, 1989.

Lee, Kyu Sik. *An Evaluation of Decentralization Policies in Light of Changing Location Patterns of Employment in the Seoul Region*. World Bank Discussion Paper No. UDD-60, 1985.

Lee, Kyu Sik. *The Location of Jobs in a Developing Metropolis: Patterns of Growth in Bogota and Cali, Colombia*. Oxford University Press, 1989.

Lee, Kyu Sik and Alex Anas. *Manufacturers' Responses to Infrastructure Deficiencies in Nigeria: Private Alternatives and Policy Options*. INU Discussion Paper No. 50, 1989.

Linn, Johannes F. *Cities in the Developing World: Policies for Their Equitable and Efficient Growth*. Oxford University Press, 1983.

Malpezzi, Stephen, Graham Tipple and Kenneth Willis. *Costs and Benefits of Rent Control in Kumasi, Ghana*. World Bank, INU Discussion Paper No. 51, 1989.

Mayo, Stephen K., Stephen Malpezzi and David J. Gross. *Shelter Strategies for the Urban Poor in Developing Countries*. World Bank Research Observer. 1986.

OECD. *Transport and the Environment*. Paris, 1988.

Silverman, Jerry M. *Public Sector Decentralization: Economic Policy Reform and Sector Investment Programs*. Mimeographed, World Bank, January 1990 (Processed).

Smith, Kirk. *Biofuels, Air Pollution and Health: A Global Review*. New York: Plenum Press, 1987.

Stren, Richard E. and Rodney R. White. *African Cities in Crisis: Managing Rapid Urban Growth*. Boulder Colorado: Westview Press, 1989.

Whittington, D., D. Lauria, and X. Mu. *Paying for Urban Services: A Study of Water Vending and Willingness to Pay in Onitsha, Nigeria*. INU Discussion Paper No. 40, 1989.

Whittington, Dale et al. *Preliminary Results of the Kumasi Sanitation Demand Study*. Mimeographed, World Bank, November 1989 (Processed).

World Bank. *World Tables 1988-89*.

World Bank. *Malaysia: The Housing Sector; Getting the Incentives Right*. Report No. 7292-MA, 1989a.

World Bank. *Ghana: Urban Sector Review*. Report No. 7384-GH, June 1989b.

World Bank. *Report on Structural Adjustment Lending II*. 1989.

World Health Organization. *The International Drinking Water Supply and Sanitation Decade: Review of Mid-Decade Progress*. Geneva, 1987.

World Health Organization. *Urbanization and its Implications for Child Health: Potential for Action*. Geneva, 1988.

www.ingramcontent.com/pod-product-compliance
Lightning Source LLC
Chambersburg PA
CBHW031522270326
41930CB00006B/491